IT AIN'T OKAY TO FAIL

AND OTHER POWERFUL LESSONS LEARNED

IN BUSINESS

by

BRIAN STRACHAN

authorHOUSE™

1663 LIBERTY DRIVE, SUITE 200
BLOOMINGTON, INDIANA 47403
(800) 839-8640
WWW.AUTHORHOUSE.COM

First published by AuthorHouse 2/23/2006

ISBN: 1-4259-0694-X (sc)
ISBN: 1-4259-0693-1 (dj)

Library of Congress Control Number: 2005910789

Printed in the United States of America
Bloomington, Indiana

This book is printed on acid-free paper.

To Juanita,
for giving me the freedom and
the space to chase my wind mills

ACKNOWLEDGEMENTS

I would like to give special thanks to Cecelia Vallaire for proof-reading the entire manuscript and offering her suggestions to strengthen the manuscript, both of which have been extremely valuable.

Dan Krinock and Dave Thomason read various chapters early in this project and provided positive feedback. I am indebted to them for their comments as well as for their encouragement to continue with this project.

Andy Bertinelli, a retired General Motors executive, reviewed several chapters and also provided strong encouragement to complete the project. During our conversations, he discussed his learning experiences at GM which were similar to mine at GE. This provided validity to the lessons I discuss in this book. I am indebted to Andy for all of his help.

Many others reviewed parts of the book and I am thankful for their comments. They include Bill Strachan, Deborah Strachan, Darin Strachan, John McCutcheon, Dan Hebert, Kevin McGlynn, Shane Walker, and Charles Higgins.

Every lesson in this book was taught to me by someone. It is difficult to recall who taught me what. When I was able to remember a particular person, I have given credit to that person. To the many others, I offer my sincere apologies for an aging and forgetful mind. Your lessons are deeply appreciated.

Special thanks go to Stephen Rabinowitz and Frank West. Both took me under their wings and made an effort to ensure that I was a better and smarter person when I left their nests.

I would also like to thank Jack Welch who, under his leadership, established a rich learning environment at GE. I learned a great deal in my years as a manager at GE during Jack's watch.

During my career I have had wonderful opportunities to broaden my experiences. Don Euhling thought this engineer could be a good sales and marketing manager. Joe Vercellotti thought this salesman would be good in manufacturing management. Dan Hebert thought I'd make a good leader on very significant projects and later entrusted me with a few of his businesses on an interim basis. Harry Franze thought I'd be a good vice president of engineering and later a vice president of sales. Bill Gradison thought I could help manage four of his successful campaigns for the U.S. Congress. I am indebted to each of you for giving me responsible opportunities in fields with which I had little or no experience, and allowing me to grow in those fields. I have enjoyed a wonderful career thanks to each of you. I feel I am truly blessed.

LESSONS LEARNED

INTRODUCTION

JUST ONE BIT OF ADVICE

Amy bounced into my office with the energy of a locomotive rolling down the tracks. Without waiting for me to look up, she blurted, "I'd like to ask you a quick question."

I liked Amy because she reminded me of my daughter Debbie. Both were highly intelligent, attractive, athletic, driven, and so full of life. They were about the same age and if you didn't know differently, you might think they were sisters.

I'll share a story about Debbie which supports my statement about the characteristics both women possessed. Spring break came not a minute too soon after a long winter in northeast Pennsylvania. Debbie got in her car and started driving south until the weather got warmer. She ended up in Kitty Hawk, North Carolina.

She saw a sign advertising hang-gliding lessons and thought that might be fun. After her first lesson ever, she had a job offer to return in the summer as a hang-gliding instructor. She accepted the offer and became an excellent instructor.

I must get back to Amy though. As she reminded me of my daughter, I am certain that I reminded her of her father. As far as Amy was concerned, I was as old as dirt (in my early fifties), said something intelligent every now and then, and was definitely not the life of the party. In fact, she called me a "piece of work" on more than one occasion. I'd always ask if that was good and she always responded, "Certainly. My dad is a piece of work also."

Amy was twenty-eight years old and was on a fast track to the top. She was Director of North American Sales for a $30 million division of a major business. She had just been promoted to general manager of another division and was leaving for that job in a few weeks.

Before I could wish her a good morning, she asked, "If you could give me just one bit of advice before I leave, what would it be?"

I thought for a while and then said, "When I was your age I also had the world by its tail. I had embarked on a promising career with GE and was identified as a high potential employee, which meant my managers felt I was capable of advancing at least two reporting levels within the company. In addition, I was a city councilman and vice-mayor in my community. Finally, I was a campaign manager for our local congressman and worked with him in Washington during a few summer vacations."

I continued, "Because of all my successes, I felt as if I knew it all. There really was no one who could teach me anything. Looking back now, I realize that I actually didn't know very much at all. I had succeeded not because of vast knowledge, but because I was driven and had a healthy dose of good luck. I know that to be true, because I've learned so much since then."

I told her, "My one bit of advice to you is to recognize that, in spite of your accomplishments, you still have a lot to learn. Understand and accept that. If nothing else, it will give you humility. You should start each morning with an objective of learning something new and end each evening by spending a few minutes reviewing what you learned that day."

I'm fairly certain that Amy left my office thinking that she should have asked for two bits of advice because the first wasn't what she was seeking. It just wasn't very profound.

I, on the other hand, felt the advice was not only profound, but was dynamite. I guess that's what made me a "piece of work".

My brief discussion with Amy has stuck with me over the years and I've recalled it many times. I have made an effort to practice it. I do try to learn something new each day and each night I try to reflect on what I've learned that day. On some days the learning comes easy. On other days, I have to make an effort to learn something. With this focus, I have learned a few things over the years. I also know that there is still a lot more to learn. Learning is a continuous process, an exciting journey that never ends.

In addition to learning, I enjoy teaching. There must be a strong "teaching" gene in my body chemistry. I used to lead a number of classes for new manufacturing managers at GE. I couldn't wait for each class to begin and hated to see each class end. It was so exciting for me to be able to stimulate the students' thought processes and to be on the receiving end of their probing questions.

A few years ago, I started thinking about all that I've learned over my career. I considered putting together an outline of lessons and heading for the local college to sell the business department on the need for a new, practical course (and perhaps a new instructor). I decided that it would be a pretty tough sell. I haven't abandoned the idea; however, I've placed it on a back burner.

My next thought was to write a book about the lessons I've learned in business. I wrote a few chapters and shared them with some colleagues. Every person responded positively and gave me encouragement to continue with the project. The seed was planted and I started the adventure in earnest.

My objective was to present a series of "lessons learned" in a simple fashion. I had no intention or desire to conduct any research. Thus, there are no scholarly charts, tables, or exhibits. Rather, you will find simple discussions of my experiences and observations over the past forty-four years in business and the lessons I've learned from them.

For the recent graduate starting a career, I hope you will find a number of hints that will help you as your career progresses. For the experienced, seasoned business person, I hope this book provides some new information to you and will give you a better insight and focus as you tackle your challenges.

One person who reviewed early portions of the book sent me the following comment:

> "What I love most about these chapters is the fact that they are simple to follow. I would imagine most people, after finishing reading your book, will feel a sense of pride in knowing that these are common sense rules which they already knew and hopefully were practicing."

When I read that statement I realized that someone else had summarized my objectives better than I had. I hope others will have a similar sense after reading this book. If so, I will have accomplished my goal.

Lesson 1

"IT AIN'T OKAY TO FAIL"

Of all the lessons I've learned in business this is the most significant. If I were to forget every lesson I learned this would be the last one that I would forget. I remember the day when Stephen Rabinowitz, a general manager at GE, lectured his staff and ended the lecture with the simple statement that, "it ain't okay to fail."

The reason I find this statement so profound is because of my own observations and experiences in American business. There is, for sure, a pervasive and prevalent culture that allows failure. It exists in most companies. I've observed it at all levels of companies from the entry-level cubicle to the boardroom. Simply stated, it's okay to fail if you have a good excuse or can blame someone else for your failure.

If you fail and can blame someone else, there is a high probability that you won't lose your job. There's even a good chance you will get your next annual pay raise and your bonus.

I admit that this culture is changing in the boardrooms with the emergence of better corporate governance and the passage of the Sarbanes-Oxley bill in the U.S. Congress. However, if one goes back only a few years and examines proxy statements they would find some

1

companies with huge annual losses and huge bonuses for the Chairmen and CEO's in the millions of dollars.

To simplify your search, look at the airline industry and remember to go back at least five years.

If you look at today's reports you will discover the huge losses are still prevalent but there are no bonuses for the executives

Companies announce guidance for the coming year. It is a range of anticipated profits divided by the number of outstanding shares. It defines the line or zone which separates success and failure. Exceed the guidance and you are a hero. Miss the guidance on the downside and you have failed, regardless of the reasons or excuses. You have failed the stockholders because Wall Street will penalize the stockholders swiftly and significantly. Yet even today with improved corporate governance, the executives of companies that failed to meet the guidance will still be rewarded with handsome salaries and bonuses.

The conclusion is simple in this case. The company misses guidance. It failed its stockholders, its owners, who lost millions of dollars of equity. The executives still get a bonus albeit possibly a reduced one. The payment of that bonus states very clearly that it's okay to fail.

It can be argued that the company missed its guidance numbers, but still made significant profits. Even though the stock tanked, the executives should be rewarded for the company's profitable performance. But it can also be argued that the same executives set the guidance. It was their number and their self-defined performance objective. If they missed their own number, they failed. Their failure cost the owners of the company, the shareholders, millions of dollars. Should the executives be lavished with million dollar bonuses when the owners collectively suffer multi-million dollar losses? Or should the executives be told that "it ain't okay to fail."?

How many meetings have you attended in which failure was discussed and ultimately excused? Have you been in a meeting like any of those below?

The CEO of Company A goes to a board meeting and has to present the bad news that revenue and profits missed estimates for the year by 5%. The discussion goes something like this. Ladies and gentlemen, it is with sincere pain that I must tell you that we have missed our revenue projections for the year by $56 million dollars or 5%. Additionally, we missed our profit projections by a commensurate amount. The reason for these shortfalls is that our sales department was far too optimistic in its estimates of the timing of the ramp-up of Ajax Company's new vehicle. And, as you know, Ajax is our major customer and accounts for over 30% of our total business."

What is going on here? The CEO unquestionably has the ultimate responsibility for the profit and loss of this company. In fact, he is highly compensated for "owning" that responsibility. However, as soon as he announced that the estimates for the year had not been met, he immediately transferred the responsibility and blame to the sales department. If he succeeds in transferring the blame to someone else, and he probably will, then the board has condoned a culture in which "it's okay for you to fail if you can blame someone else for the failure."

Now let us look at Company B. The vice president of manufacturing is reviewing the start-up of a new product with the president of the company. He states, "It looks like we will finally be in production in five more weeks".

The president responds with, "that's good news; however, we promised our distributors that we'd have product in their hands three weeks ago. If your estimate is correct, we're going to be at least two months late".

The vice president responds, "I understand, but when you consider that engineering was three months late with a final design, I think my people have performed admirably in cutting our losses".

This vice president is a little more politically astute. Again, there is a failure in the corporate process. Again, the person responsible for getting product into the hands of the distributors has not met his objectives. Again, it is okay for him to fail because he can direct the blame to someone else. In fact, in the same breath that he is affixing the blame, he is taking credit for minimizing the failure. Incredibly, he is turning a failure into a victory. Again, we see that it's okay to fail.

There is no data to allow us to quantify the prevalence of this culture in American business. There is no data to allow us to quantify how rampant it exists in any particular company. There is no data because most companies don't even recognize that this culture does exist. Believe me, it has existed in 100% of the companies for which I have toiled, including GE. As nearly as I can tell from my various vantage points in those companies, it existed at all levels of the organization. If the culture exists at the top, why wouldn't it exist throughout the entire organization?

I watched Stephen Rabinowitz reverse this culture in a department at GE. In doing so, he impacted my thought processes for the rest of my career.

Stephen had been our general manager for about a month. We were having a staff meeting to review the status of several major projects. It seemed as if every time an objective was being reviewed, the objective had not been met, and the person responsible started to explain who was to blame. After about four projects, Stephen calmly said, "You are telling me you failed and that your failure is acceptable because it wasn't your fault. Before you go any further, I must tell you, "it ain't okay to fail in this department."

He continued by repeating, "all of you must understand that it ain't okay to fail. The next time a person tells me that engineering failed to have a design completed on time, I am going to ask engineering what that person did to help them meet their objectives. If you think manufacturing was responsible for a failure, you better have done all you could to help them identify and solve their problems. Does anyone have any questions?"

We all knew he was very serious about what he said and there were no questions. However, just to make sure none of us forgot the new culture, he repeated those five little words one more time, "It ain't okay to fail."

His simply stated edict had a significant impact on all of us. We became obsessed with becoming "winners". We started building a Super Bowl management team. We started working together better than we ever dreamed. We began asking each other how their assignments were going. We wondered if there was anything we could do to help each other. We became one dynamite staff. We started having fewer and fewer failures. We started to better appreciate each other's strengths.

Five little words delivered strongly two or three times helped us become a team of winners.

Perhaps more significantly, we each explained to each of our staffs that, "it ain't okay to fail."

Again, this is a culture. It is a culture that must be established to maximize everyone's performance. When it permeates the organization the business results improve dramatically.

"It ain't okay to fail" is a philosophy that needs to be practiced by the individual contributor, the CEO, and everyone in between. More importantly, it is a culture that must be established in American businesses. When it is, those businesses will do nothing but improve.

Isn't it ridiculous that an engineer fails, blames someone else for the failure, and gets a nice pay raise? Isn't it absurd that a top executive fails, blames the bad national economy, and still gets a multi-million dollar bonus? These examples are ridiculous, absurd, and very real.

"It ain't okay to fail" isn't contentious and shouldn't be debatable. It should simply be a part of the business culture.

If you are an individual contributor, adopt the philosophy. Keep it in the front of your mind as you perform your assignments. Use your brain and energy avoiding failures instead of looking for excuses. Live the philosophy.

If you are an executive, articulate the philosophy. Do exactly what Stephen Rabinowitz did at GE. Syndicate the philosophy throughout the organization and watch the results improve.

If you choose to adopt this culture for your organization, there are three things you must do. You must articulate it over and over again, you must personally establish the objectives, and you must not reward failure.

Articulate that it ain't okay to fail at every opportunity. Instruct your staff members to do the same with their reports. Hammer at it until everyone in the organization understands it.

Next, you must take control of goal setting. If the individual knows that failure is unacceptable and is allowed to set his own objectives, you can be certain that those goals will be risk-aversive. A good example is the annual budgeting process. The sales team sandbags their sales forecasts, usually making them lower than is realistic in order to enhance their odds of making the forecast.

You, as the business leader, must set the objectives or anticipate a lot of sandbagging. However, goal setting must be a collaborative exercise with the person or organization which will own the goals and be measured by their success in achieving them. Part of the goals may not be negotiable. At GE, we were expected to deliver cost productivity of 6% every year and that goal was not negotiable. Some goals should be negotiable. Perhaps you are too aggressive in your timeline and the engineer explains that some things can't be done as quickly as you want. At GE, we designed and built manufacturing equipment. Some items required castings that took 20 weeks to obtain. There was no way they could be accelerated and setting an objective of anything less than 20 weeks was setting up a certain failure.

Discuss the objectives before carving them in concrete. Be aggressive in setting the goals, listen to the arguments, and make your decision.

Finally, establish a reward system and make sure everyone understands it. Make sure you reward the people who make their goals. And make sure you don't reward the person who fails.

Really, it shouldn't be okay to fail, should it? In my experience, it really hasn't been tough to establish a culture in which it ain't okay to fail.

Lesson 2

FAILURES WILL HAPPEN

"It ain't okay to fail" does not mean you will never fail. There will be times when you do fail no matter how hard you try to win. If you accept the concept that "it ain't okay to fail" you will be upset with yourself if you do fail. You should try to learn lessons from failures and not repeat the same mistakes.

Abraham Lincoln is regarded as one of our greatest presidents. He is credited with saving the Union. Prior to winning the presidency, Mr. Lincoln ran for the state legislature, the House of Representatives, the Senate, and the vice-presidency. He failed to win election to each of these positions at one time or another. However, he didn't accept failure but learned from each. In the end he won the presidency and became one of our greatest presidents.

The 1998 Yankees had the best record in the history of baseball. They still walked off the field as losers - 50 times!

Thomas Edison, perhaps the greatest inventor of all time, tried hundreds of materials and compounds and failed hundreds of times before he discovered the combination of materials that would work as a filament for a light bulb.

For decades, Babe Ruth held the record for most home-runs. The year he set that record, he led in another statistic – most strike-outs. If you swing for the fence to get the maximum results, it is a fact that you will strike out many times.

In his book *Winning*, Jack Welch, the former Chairman of GE, admits that he failed on numerous occasions. He learned from each failure. In spite of his failures, Fortune magazine named him the best CEO of the 20th Century.

What these examples demonstrate is that our country's greatest successes have also had failures along the way. Failure was not okay with them. But they learned from them and went forward to succeed.

Many times the difference between winning and failing is the definition of the objective. Edison's objective was to invent a light bulb. The fact that he tried hundreds of times before succeeding does not mean he failed hundreds of times. These were but potholes along the road to success, which was defined as inventing a light bulb. In the end, he accomplished his goal and succeeded.

The objective of a professional football team is to win the Super Bowl. During the game, they may have some fumbles and interceptions. They may even be losing for three quarters but finish the game as the winning team. While they may have had setbacks along the way, they didn't fail in the ultimate objective.

When adopting the philosophy and establishing the culture of "it ain't okay to fail" it is important that you clearly understand the ultimate objective. Having done that, strive relentlessly to meet that objective and don't be deterred by potholes along the way.

You will fail from time to time. Accept it. Take responsibility for it and don't blame others. Learn from it. Don't expect to be rewarded for it. And move on to your next challenge.

Lesson 3

"IF YOU ASK ME TO LIE FOR YOU TODAY..."

My friend Jerry Barnes told me of a young lady he observed early in his career.

She had recently graduated from high school and was in her first week working as a secretary.

One day her manager told her, "I don't want to be disturbed for an hour. If anyone calls for me, tell them I'm out of the office."

She thought for a few seconds and said, "I will do as you ask. But, if you ask me to lie <u>for</u> you today, how long do you think it will be before I lie <u>to</u> you?"

Wow!

* * * *

Do not ask your employees to lie or to compromise their values in any way, shape, or form.

If you can't think of a way to ask your secretary to hold your calls, without asking her to tell a lie in the process, you need to find another job which doesn't require using the telephone.

We look for employees with honesty, values, and character. When we get employees with these virtues, we should do nothing to compromise them.

Lesson 4

HONESTY AND INTEGRITY

In all you do in life and in business, do it with complete honesty, strong values, and integrity. The rewards may not happen immediately, but they will come in time. Conversely, if you lack honesty and integrity the consequences will ultimately hurt you.

As we entered the 21st Century, we saw a wave of business scandals unfold. The scandals were perpetrated by a small number of business leaders who apparently lacked honesty and integrity. Their actions ultimately hurt them as well as thousands of innocent people.

The Enron Corporation, an energy trading, natural gas, and electric utilities giant, became the largest corporate failure in history when it filed for Chapter 11 protection in December, 2001. It also became the "poster boy" for corporate fraud.

A few weeks after it filed for bankruptcy, the United States Department of Justice announced that it was going to pursue a criminal investigation of Enron.

Enron's problems evolved from questionable accounting procedures which bordered on fraud. It came to light that much of Enron's revenues and profits came from deals with limited partnerships which it controlled. As a result, many of Enron's losses were not reported in its financial statements.

As the scandal unfolded, Enron's stock dropped from $85 a share to 30-cents. Thousands of investors lost billions of dollars, including large portions of their retirement plans. Loyal employees suffered the same fate because their business leaders chose a path of dishonesty and fraud.

Those business leaders are also suffering their consequences, arguably in a less painful manner than the financially-broken investors. Former CFO, Andrew Fastow was indicted on 78 counts of fraud, money laundering, and conspiracy. He was found guilty, sentenced to 10 years in prison, and had to forfeit $23.8 million in personal assets. Kenneth Lay, former Chairman, and Jeffrey Skilling, former CEO, have both been indicted for their part in the scandal and are scheduled for trial in January 2006.

Enron is not the only business that has failed in recent years because of a few executives who didn't subscribe to honest and ethical behavior. There are other companies that have practiced fraudulent behavior. They are all well documented elsewhere.

Collectively, those business leaders have launched the need for far-reaching, new federal legislation pertaining to corporate governance and accounting practices. Shame on all of these leaders for what they've done to their companies, to their loyal investors, and to American business as an entity.

Honesty and strong values are not the best policy; they should be the only policy. Whatever is gained by a lack of honesty is usually short-lived and will evaporate in time.

* * * *

Long ago, my then ten-year old son asked me to lend him some money to start a baseball card business. After reviewing his plans I proudly invested $800 in his little business. I also became an employee. At his age, he needed someone to drive the station wagon to card shows and to help carry the heavy cases of cards. He hired me to do those jobs.

As an aside, I can't help myself from bragging about this little venture. After two years of card shows, we leased a small retail store in our community's town square. We opened the store after school three days a week and on Saturdays. Even with those limited hours of operation, we grew the business to annual revenues exceeding $100,000 with respectable margins, and sold it for a handsome gain when he turned sixteen and developed other interests.

Helping my son run his business gave me countless opportunities to teach him about customer service, quality, commitments, and ethics. Honesty became our hallmark and it returned countless benefits, including financial results. I need to tell you about our experience with Jimmy.

We were located in an affluent community and enjoyed having some of Cleveland's professional athletes and coaches as customers.

One day at dinner my son Darin told me that he had short-changed Jimmy. Jimmy was the trainer for the Cleveland Indians. He had purchased some cards that day, had given my son a fifty-dollar bill and Darin gave him change for a twenty. Darin discovered the fifty dollar bill the next time he opened the cash register. He grabbed thirty dollars and headed out on the street to find Jimmy. Unfortunately Jimmy was long gone.

None of our customers knew where Jimmy lived and we discovered he had an unlisted phone number. We put thirty dollars in an envelope to give to Jimmy the next time he came into the shop. Three weeks passed and we never saw Jimmy.

We did have tickets to all the Indians' home games on Sundays. We decided to go to the next game a little early and vowed to find Jimmy.

We were able to locate the clubhouse at the stadium and asked the guard to tell Jimmy we were outside.

When he came out, we told him that we accidentally short-changed him and he told us that we were indeed correct. He had a fifty and a twenty in his pocket when he came into the shop and thought he gave us the twenty. Later that day, he went to dinner and discovered he had the twenty-dollar bill in his pocket, not the fifty. We asked why he didn't come back to the store and tell us that we short-changed him. He told us that he didn't think we would believe him.

We apologized for the mistake and gave him thirty dollars. It was obvious that he was impressed with our honesty. It became more apparent when he invited Darin to come into the clubhouse and meet the players before the game started. What a thrill for a kid who loved baseball, and particularly, the Cleveland Indians. What a thrill for a dad who wanted his children to have great life experiences. And what a great real-life lesson about honesty and integrity.

As we headed to our seats I told my son he could have pocketed the thirty dollars. If he did so, he would probably lose a very good customer. He could have returned the money, as he did, and got no more than a thank-you for his effort, which would have been just fine. But in this case, he earned the respect of another person and got a fabulous reward for his honesty. This was a great lesson for my son to learn and a great way to learn it. In the long run, honesty and integrity have a way of being rewarded.

In business and in life, always be honest, have strong values, and show good character. If you get no other reward than the respect of others, you will know that you are a winner.

If you find yourself in a business where you fear some of your management is dishonest or lacks integrity, my advice is to get out of that business. Some day, a manager who lacks values may need an excuse for one of his failures and you may find yourself "thrown in the bag" as the excuse for the failure. It's just not worth it to work for anyone who lacks basic integrity.

* * * *

I am currently employed with Leggett and Platt ("L&P"), a Fortune 500 company headquartered in Carthage, Missouri. You may never have heard of L&P, but you probably have some of our components in the products you use. We make components for bedding, furniture, gas grills, automobiles, motor cycles, and a host of other products you can find in your home or garage.

Leggett and Platt is led by two men, Felix Wright and Dave Haffner. Both of these gentlemen possess the strong values found in the company's mid-west location. They are honest, hard-working men who truly care about the people in the Leggett and Platt family. I am very proud of my company and its leaders.

Felix and Dave lead by example in the areas of honesty and integrity. They also expect their employees to follow that example. Each year they publish a booklet entitled "Business Policies Manual." The introduction says it all:

> "Companies are known by the reputation their employees earn. Through the years our Company and its employee-partners have earned a reputation for honesty and integrity. Together we have built an excellent reputation with our customers, suppliers, shareholders, regulators, the communities we serve and the general public."

> "As an employee-partner you share the obligation to protect and strengthen our hard-earned reputation. This Business Policies Manual is your guide to ethical and lawful conduct and serves as a reminder of the policies, rules and laws that govern our performance."

I have pride that my business leaders have values. I am happy that they insist that my colleagues and I share the same values. I am certain that they are sincere in their demands for honesty and integrity throughout the entire organization.

I also gage a company's values by how much the leaders care about the employees. It is well known that only a handful of major businesses have pension plans that are fully funded. That says there are only a few companies that can absolutely guarantee your pension will be there when you retire and need it. I am proud and happy that my company is one of those few.

That tells me a lot about my company and its leaders. More importantly, it tells me that my company "cares" about its employees and doesn't compromise the pension funding for the sake of making the business look better to its shareholders. It has values because its leaders have values. That is the kind of company I want to work for and the type of leaders I admire. They have integrity and it shows.

* * * *

I want to say a few words about Jack Welch, the former chairman of GE. Part of Jack's brilliance was his ability to take something complex and syndicate it into something simple that could not be misunderstood.

He developed a simple, four-block matrix to evaluate GE people. Which block you landed in was based on only two factors – your performance to agreed-upon objectives and your values.

Jack defined values as behaviors. These behaviors, or values, included virtuous factors but also included the behaviors you needed to achieve your objectives.

If you fell into the block with strong performance and strong values, you were eligible for promotion. If you were in the block for weak performance and weak values, you needed to be looking for another job immediately. If you landed in one of the other two boxes, which meant you were strong in one category but not the other, management had a tough decision to make regarding your future.

This simple assessment was applied to all employees, regardless of where they were on the corporate ladder. I personally knew one high-level executive who was fired even though his business had good results. While he achieved those results, he did so with values that didn't measure up to the GE standards and the decision was made to let him go.

If your company doesn't explicitly give you a grade for honesty, values, and character, you can be sure that they are factors in shaping your performance. Having them will enhance your performance and will help make you a success.

Be honest in all you do. Have integrity and let it show. It will help you be successful in life and in business.

Lesson 5

WHAT DO YOU WANT TO DO WHEN YOU GROW UP?

Every now and then one of our less-experienced employees will ask me for advice regarding his or her career. Usually the person has been offered another job and he is asking whether that opportunity would be good for his career.

I love to get requests for career counseling because I enjoy working with the less experienced people and I believe that I can help them.

I usually start the discussion by stressing that I can't answer the question because I don't know anything about their career or their goals. I don't know what they want to achieve during their career and thus can't tell them whether the new opportunity will help or hurt them. If you don't know your destination, any old road will get you there.

I then ask, "What do you want to do when you grow up?" Some people know exactly what they want to achieve during their careers. They are few and far between. Most of the people haven't spent a whole lot of time thinking about their specific career goals and particularly what position they hope to hold as retirement approaches.

21

The latter are stunned when I tell that them that career counseling begins with your obituary. After the initial look of disbelief I say, "Seriously, when you pass on and someone is writing your obituary, what do you want to be remembered for? Is it that you were the CEO of a Fortune 500 company? Or perhaps that you owned your own business? Or is it something else such as you were a Congressman or the leader of a Scouting organization or the author of a best-selling cookbook? Only when you define your destination, can I help you choose the path you need to take to reach it."

Throughout all of my career counseling sessions I have stressed to the individual that it is your career, not mine. You are the only person who can decide whether a particular opportunity will help you along your career path. All I can do is give you questions that you must answer to help you reach your decision.

I'll always remember the advice I gave a colleague in one of our businesses. It was a very small business with approximately $3 million in annual sales. The staff was small and most wore more than one hat. This fellow was handling both the sales and human resources functions. The business was growing, it had reached $6 million in sales, and was heading upward. It was decided that the business needed a full-time sales manager and a full-time human resources manager. My friend had to decide fairly quickly which of the two positions he wanted and he sought my advice.

We went through the obituary discussion and he told me that his career goals were to someday run a business. Having defined his goal, I gave him a simple exercise to help him make his decision. I suggested that he go to the library or the Internet and research the abbreviated biographies of some Fortune 500 CEO's. I told him to keep track of how many reached that position by following a path in sales and how many followed a path in human resources. That exercise would help him decide which path to take to help him achieve his goals

The lesson here is that you need to research the paths taken by people who have achieved the goals you have. That will help you decide which path you should take to meet your career objectives.

Remember always that it is your career and insist that the decisions impacting your career are yours to make.

Lesson 6

ARE YOUR STRENGTHS UNDER CONTROL?

I first learned of this particular concept of strengths and excesses in the context of annual performance appraisals. Periodic performance feedback, coupled with an annual performance appraisal, is an integral part of a well-run business. Honest appraisals which inform the employee of his or her development needs are critical to helping the employee improve. They also help the business improve because its employees are improving their performance. It's a "win-win" proposition.

Unfortunately, not all appraisals are honest. The one for the outstanding employee is easy to conduct and is a pleasure. The one for the marginal employee can be difficult because the discussion can become argumentative and contentious. I have seen too many managers avoid the tough performance appraisal by simply deeming an employee's performance to be satisfactory and avoiding any discussion of development needs.

This is unacceptable because it is unfair to the marginal employee. Sooner or later the true assessment will come to light and it will be a shock to the employee. Perhaps it will come in the form of a layoff notice. Perhaps it will come with a new manager who believes in giving honest performance assessments. Whatever the form, the day will come and it won't be pretty.

I never understood why many managers don't give honest appraisals. Again, the employee deserves honest feedback. If a manager can't conduct an honest discussion, he should not accept a position as a manager.

In one particular staff discussion this subject was being discussed. The general manager stated that he expected his managers to conduct honest performance appraisals with their people. He further stated that there is no need for the discussions with marginal employees to be contentious if the discussion is in terms of strengths and excesses.

The theory he was discussing is that no one inherently has any weaknesses. We develop weaknesses when we carry strengths to an excess.

Self confidence is a trait we admire, we strive to have, and we count as a strength. If we carry the strength of self-confidence to an excess, it becomes arrogance, and a weakness.

Consider one's ability to trust others. This is a strength and one which you need to develop as you need to delegate more to others. If you carry trust to an excess it becomes gullibility.

Being strong and forceful are strengths.
Carry them to an excess and you become a bully.

Being cautious is a strength. Carry it an excess and you become indecisive.

Being cooperative is a strength. Carry it to an excess and you become a pushover.

Taking risks is a strength and a necessary ingredient to being an entrepreneur. If you carry risk-taking to an excess you can become reckless.

Having ambition is a strength. In this case I'm thinking of the person with the desire and ambition to get ahead. You've recognized that in some people and you admire their drive. However, I have seen some people carry their ambition to an excess. They become obsessed with getting ahead and start doing some pretty dumb things which have hurt their chances. They carried their strength right into a weakness.

Again, this was presented in the context of having performance discussions with marginal people in a positive manner.

Like many of the lessons I've learned I have thought about them long after and have extrapolated them beyond their original context. In this case I have tried to self-assess my weaknesses to see if they are indeed strengths carried to an excess. Not surprisingly, the theory fits the case.

I feel one of my strengths is the capacity to speak out when I don't agree with something being said. In other words, I am not a "yes-person." I think of this as a strength which adds value to the organization.

In my later years I came to the realization that this strength was of value to me if I utilized it in moderation. If I carry my outspokenness to an excess I become argumentative. I have learned to speak out more sparingly and with more caution. I will speak out when I think something is wrong or if I think something can be done in a better way. However, I don't play devil's advocate as much as I used to and I've learned to pick my fights.

I think it is a very healthy exercise for everyone to periodically make a list of his or her strengths. You should know yourself pretty well and should be able to easily list your strengths. Which of your characteristics make you proud? What do you do well and which characteristics contribute to your doing that well?

Once you have your list spend some time thinking about what those characteristics would become if they were carried to an excess. Then ask yourself, "is there any characteristic on the list that I might be carrying to an excess? Are any of these strengths becoming weaknesses?" If there are, you need to consider what you are going to do about them.

From time to time you must ask yourself, "are my strengths under control?"

Lesson 7

DON'T BE A "YES" PERSON BUT PROCEED WITH CAUTION

This lesson follows from my admitted strength of outspokenness carried to an excess.

In Jack Welch's book *Winning* he spends some time discussing candor. He states that, for a business to be successful there must be candor. Candor means brutal honesty, telling it like it is, and not being shy about it. His career was marked by outspoken candor and it served him well. He admits that his performance appraisals usually said that he was abrasive, but he was so strong that his abrasiveness never harmed his advancement. While he recommends the brutal style of candor, he does admit that many may not be able to pull it off as he did in his career.

Everyone should be honest and candid as Jack insists. Businesses need candor and debates in order to not pursue the wrong path. Unlike Jack, I think that candor needs to be presented cautiously. Some managers can handle the "in-your face" style and enjoy the ensuing debates. Far more managers have no capacity for it.

Almost every leader for whom I have worked has announced that he does not want to have "yes" people on his staff. I have always taken this statement at face value and challenged my leaders when I felt there was a better way to do things. This has, in many cases, been a costly mistake and has not served me well over my career.

A leader who surrounds himself with "yes" people has a business which is being run sub-optimally. If the staff doesn't have the ability to question the leader from time to time then the business is utilizing only one brain to set the course. Every leader knows this and announces that he doesn't want "yes" people and expects everyone to speak up and question decisions.

I have come to believe that what most leaders want is for their people to speak up; however, they neglect to say that they don't want you speaking up in front of the rest of the staff. They really don't want any questioning or challenges in front of an audience. In spite of what they say, when you do speak up, the leader gets defensive, the discussion becomes contentious, and you end up losing the argument.

This is not always the case. One general manager encouraged speaking up and seemed to thrive on discussions even if they got heated. Great ideas were exchanged and debated. We came out of meetings, usually in concert with each other, and got outstanding results in that business.

It was fun to participate in those meetings. The general manager got a lot of challenges to his decisions. Sometimes he would raise his hand in the middle of the debate and say, "I've listened to your ideas, we're becoming redundant and it's time to vote. The vote is a tie and my vote becomes the tie-breaker". We'd all laugh and move on to the next subject. But we all felt good because we had the opportunity to present our ideas and we felt as if we were providing added value to the business. Every now and then he would raise his hand to signal the debate was over and he would announce the vote was overwhelmingly in our favor. We won some votes, we lost some votes, and in total had a great time.

Another business that I participated in wanted debates and challenges only on certain decisions. The leader would usually announce his decisions and discussions centered on the details of the decision. Every now and then he would say, "It's okay to push back on this decision". The first time I heard this statement I wondered what he meant. I quickly learned that he was announcing the fact that he wasn't sure about the decision and he was inviting discussion and debate.

All others who professed that they wanted open debate and discussion really didn't mean it. It's as if they regarded questioning and debate as an attack on them.

One manager who invited debate would actually stare down anyone who challenged anything in his meetings. He would not say a word when anyone commented and he would just stare at the person menacingly for what seemed like a long time. Everyone learned quickly to not challenge or debate a thing he said.

This manager moved on and a replacement was named. The funny thing was that he later told someone that he was surprised with the selection of his replacement because the replacement seemed like such a "yes" man. He didn't have a clue that he had forced everyone on his staff to be a "yes" man.

As I mentioned, speaking up has not served me well over the years. I'm a slow learner and have finally come to the conclusion that I need to watch my colleagues in meetings and assess how seriously a manger is when he says he doesn't want "yes" people.

I do recommend that everyone should speak up when they see an alternate path to something which may have a better payback. I also recommend that you speak up carefully. Pick a time and place which is not threatening and which doesn't challenge the manager in front of others.

If you attend a meeting and determine that you have a better idea, wait for the meeting to end. Afterwards, when you are alone with the manager, tell him that you've been thinking of a particular statement. Tell him that it was a great idea and that, as you've thought it through, you feel that an alternative approach might have a better payback. Come from the direction that there's more than one way to get to the destination and ask if he's considered the alternate route that you're thinking about. Make sure to reiterate that there's nothing wrong with his approach, that you agree with it, but your approach might just get there quicker or have better results. Again, the discussion has to be one-on-one so as not to be threatening.

It is important that you get your ideas considered. You are being paid to add value to your business. Your ideas are part of the added-value you bring to the organization.

Once you've had the opportunity to present and discuss an idea, the manager will make a decision. Once that decision is announced, you must recognize that all debate is finished. If your alternative is not accepted, your job becomes very simple. You must do your best and give your all to seeing that your manager's path is followed and it is followed to a successful conclusion. You must do that if for no other reason that "it ain't okay to fail".

Lesson 8

NEVER BE AFRAID TO ASK DUMB QUESTIONS

It was the autumn of 1963. I was a cooperative education student (a co-op) on a work quarter employed by the Naval Ship R&D Center in Washington, D.C. We were feverishly preparing for a visit by President Kennedy in early December. It was Friday afternoon and I was already looking forward to the weekend.

At about 1:30 the paging system activated and the Commander delivered a brief, somber message. He announced, "I have just received word that President Kennedy and Governor Connally have been shot in Dallas. As I receive more reports, I will keep you posted. All of us need to pray for them".

Everyone went into shock. Small groups formed to pray, to comfort each other, and to talk about the two men. Others walked aimlessly in offices and halls, alone with their thoughts.

Later in the afternoon, the Commander again spoke to tell us that President Kennedy had died. He also told us that Governor Connally's wounds were not severe and that he would recover. The shock got worse and many tears flowed. Seasoned naval officers, veterans of war, joined others with tears of grief.

The strong emotions of that afternoon were, however, conflicting. While there was genuine grief and tears for the President, there was equally genuine joy for the Governor. I was upset that the President had been assassinated. To me, it was a horrible, despicable action. I was glad the Governor would recover, but couldn't understand why my colleagues were so emotional over a governor in a state so far away. It bothered me that I was missing something. I didn't understand the intensity of the feelings for the Governor.

I saw Frank West sitting in his office. Frank was the senior manager in the department and had been a father-figure to me. I went into his office and said, "I'm almost afraid to ask this question because it may seem dumb, but I will anyway".

I then proceeded to tell Frank that while I understood the shock and grief for losing President Kennedy, I didn't quite understand why everyone was as concerned, if not more so, for Governor Connally.

Frank explained that John Connally prior to becoming Govermor of Texas had served as the Secretary of the Navy. He had been a good secretary, had helped our base, and had even visited on two occasions. He was a very friendly person and had taken the time to meet and chat with a number of people in our department. To many, John Kennedy was the president, but John Connally was perceived as a friend! That is why so many were concerned about the Govenor.

Before I left his office he said, "Brian, as you go through life do not ever be afraid to ask dumb questions."

I have heeded his advice for over forty years. Has it hurt me? Perhaps in a case or two it has. Whenever it has hurt me, I am aware of it, have learned from those experiences, and am a better person because of it.

Has it helped me? I'm certain that it has on many occasions. It has given me knowledge that I needed at the time and otherwise would not have obtained.

We are reluctant to ask dumb questions because we fear that they may make us look dumb. In my case in November 1963, I assumed that my question was a dumb one. It wasn't perceived as being dumb because I didn't work for the Navy Department when John Connally was Secretary of the Navy. I had little opportunity to know that fact. Frank West knew I had recently joined the Navy Department and, to him, my question didn't seem dumb at all.

As I mentioned, a few questions have backfired and have not helped me. From them, I've learned two rules.

First, when you ask a dumb question, consider your setting. If you are in a meeting with more than one other person, hold your question until the meeting is over. Ask one person your question later. There is just no advantage in asking your question in front of a group.

Second, ask your question to someone you trust and who respects you. That person knows you are not dumb and your dumb question will not change that opinion.

* * * *

Never be afraid to ask a dumb question. You probably need to know the answer. Follow the two simple rules above and you'll never be hurt by asking.

<u>Lesson 9</u>

EVERY DECISION YOU MAKE IS CORRECT

Some people have no difficulty making decisions. In fact, they seem to enjoy making decisions.

A number of other people seem to have a great deal of difficulty in making decisions. I think their reluctance is based on a fear of making a bad decision.

Decision making can be complex. There are entire books devoted to the subject. I once participated in a week long course in decision making. While it can be complex, it doesn't necessarily need to be.

One day I was discussing this subject with another manager. Unfortunately, I do not recall who that person was. We were discussing the fact that we had people working for us who just couldn't make a simple decision. My colleague said, "It's really a shame because every decision you make is correct". When I asked him to elaborate he told me that every decision you make is correct, based upon the facts that you have at the time you make the decision. Ten minutes after making the decision the world can change and your decision may look incorrect. But at the time you made it, it was correct.

Adopting this philosophy, decision making becomes easy because there is no such thing as a bad decision. I have come to believe in that concept. While I had no trouble making a decision at the time, I think of that often and decision making has become even easier.

I have had many opportunities to teach this lesson to many people over my career and each person became more comfortable with making decisions. One example of this was with my young son in his baseball card business.

We read in trade journals that hockey cards had become popular and we ordered a case of hockey cards for about $500. We lived in the greater Cleveland, Ohio area. At the time, Cleveland didn't have a hockey team. While the cards were hot in some areas, they weren't in Cleveland. Our case of cards sat on the shelf for over a year with practically no sales.

Each week day when I came home from work we discussed that day's baseball card business over dinner. Darin was about fourteen years old at the time and opened the card shop after school with his mother for a few hours each day. He knew the business and had full authority to make deals, some of which exceeded a thousand dollars. It was his business.

One particular evening he told me he thought he had made a bad decision. Someone from Pittsburgh, the home of the NHL Penguins, came into the shop looking for hockey cards. When he saw that we weren't selling them at a premium over their suggested retail price he asked how many cards we had and offered $800 for the case. Darin accepted the offer.

Later in the day he discovered that those cases were selling for $1,000. He assumed that he could have sold them for more than he did and concluded he had made a bad decision.

I told him he made the correct decision at the time and I was delighted. The most important fact was that they had no market value in Cleveland and were essentially worthless to us. He not only got our money back but made a 60% gross profit. It was fantastic and I praised him for his decision.

I told him that every decision he would make would be correct based on the facts he has at the time he makes it, and this decision was no different. The facts may change ten minutes later, but that didn't matter. In his case it appeared as if he could have made more money had he been aware of the national selling price average. However, if he tried to get that, the man from Pittsburgh may have decided he could buy the cards at home for that price. We'll never know that for sure. We also will never know if he pushed for a higher price whether those cards and the $500 would still be sitting on our shelf.

The message is clear. Make the best decision you can based on the facts that you have at hand. Realize that it was the correct decision and don't waste any time second-guessing it because new facts came to light afterwards. Spend that time climbing another mountain and making different decisions. You will enjoy life a lot more.

Darin agreed and I never again heard him say that he might have made a bad decision. I don't believe he ever did make a bad decision.

Lesson 10

DO SOMETHING THAT NO ONE ELSE DOES

A few years ago someone told me, "to become invaluable to your employer, do something that no one else does."

It is implied in this message that the "something" has value to your employer.

I pondered this advice for some time. I thought back over my career and searched for instances in which I may have benefited from this advice without ever realizing it. My conclusion was that I had done this a few times with very favorable personal results.

The most significant instance that I recall was a period in my career when I became a unique resource person. I could go into our manufacturing plants which were experiencing problems and I could identify the true root causes of those problems. Better yet, I could identify the root causes rapidly, usually within twenty-four hours.

Typical problems were missing delivery commitments to customers, manufacturing costs exceeding goals or standards, and other things that might be hurting the business results. Usually, the numbers told

41

everyone that the reason was something like high scrap, high downtime, high absenteeism, or something else along those lines. But, in most cases, no one could identify the real reasons for the high scrap, downtime, or absenteeism.

To this day, I vividly remember my first assignment as a troubleshooter. But first, I need to point out something different about yesteryear's culture. People from the home office always wore their three-piece, pin-striped suits when visiting factories. I didn't adhere to this practice because it was a good way to ruin an expensive suit. If I got within twenty feet of grease, it seemed to find a way to jump onto my clothing. My preferred "uniform" in a plant was jeans, a sweatshirt, safety shoes, safety glasses, and ear plugs.

One day my manager asked me to go to our Memphis Lamp Plant to try to discover why it was taking seven days a week to make shipments of a new tail lamp for Ford. The daily shipments required overnight air shipments to Atlanta every evening in order to keep from shutting down Ford's assembly line.

I was not well known in Memphis and arrived at the plant in jeans and a sweatshirt in the middle of the evening shift. Too late to meet the plant manager, I decided to wander around the manufacturing floor and see what I could learn.

Within an hour, I came across a lamp-making machine that quickly caught my attention. It was idle and its operator was comfortably leaning back in a chair with her feet propped up on the table. I quickly approached the operator.

I didn't introduce myself and I'm certain that she assumed I was not a manager, but rather a new colleague from another area of the plant on a break. As I approached I smiled and said, "I'd like to have a job like yours".

She quickly told me that they had to produce so many lamps a week for the customer. If it took five days she made her base pay. If it took six days, she made more money. If it took seven days, she made a lot more money. With Christmas coming, everyone in the plant needed extra money.

I'll never forget her answer to my question about how do you get the machine to "go down" without getting caught. She said, "There are 101 ways to make that happen and the clowns up front don't have a clue to what's happening". She was correct; however, I thought to myself that the "clowns" would know a little more by tomorrow.

I spent the rest of the night sitting in the break room. I blended in with the others as I carefully listened to scores of discussions. Quite a few conversations were about Christmas and the need for more money to buy presents for loved ones.

At no time during the evening did anyone ask me who I was. Had they, I would have been completely honest. I would have told them I was from Nela Park (headquarters) and was in the plant to find out why it took so long to make the new lamps for Ford.

The next day, I gave my findings and recommendations to the plant manager and flew home to accolades from my manager. I was praised for my good work and for the speed with which I had accomplished it.

I soon got a similar assignment and then another and yet another. By dressing in jeans and sweatshirt, sitting in the break room on off-shifts, drinking too many cups of coffee, and listening, I quickly understood what was really happening in the plant. Within twenty-four hours, I could correctly identify the root causes of problems and make sound recommendations for rapid solutions.

I actually reached a point where I was going to plants that weren't even in our division. I had stumbled into something I could do and no one else could. In doing so, I had become invaluable to my business. I had become a resource person.

I want to add that all problems were not caused by the rank and file. I discovered that problems can also be caused by dumb things done by management or direction given by management. You can be sure that the rank and file are aware of those things and discuss them at length.

In my example here, it can be argued that others could have done the same thing that I did. I admit that others could have done it, if only they knew how. It didn't require rocket science. It did involve shedding the three-piece suit, which no one would think of doing in those times. It involved sitting in break rooms for hours on end which no one would have equated to meaningful work.

* * * *

Doing something that no one else does or can do is a "lesson learned" and can become part of your personal strategy. How to go about it or to develop the tactics to satisfy the strategy is a challenge.

In my example, I "lucked" into it.

My attempts at developing a nice list of things that you can do to become a unique resource person have been fruitless.

You know your own circumstances and your business environment. Both will dictate how you proceed with the lesson of this chapter.

You can look around for problems being suffered by your business, activities that are not being done well, or functions which are not being performed and would have value if they were. Give some thought to what you could do to solve the problem, improve the activity, or perform the function.

If you hit on something, develop a mental plan and start to execute it. If you are comfortable with your manager, share your thoughts and get concurrence to execute your plan.

These hints are in no case comprehensive. You will have to develop a lot more by yourself.

As you proceed, keep in mind that you usually can succeed with something very simple.

You want to succeed because "it ain't okay to fail".

Lesson 11

LOOK FOR PROBLEMS AND HELP SOLVE THEM

Becoming a solid resource person is a great way of enhancing success along your career path. Doing something that no one else does is a good way to become a resource person. Finding problems and helping to solve them is another way. People who solve problems get noticed.

I spent my first six years at GE as a systems engineer working on a newly designed aircraft engine for large commercial airplanes. I stayed with that engine through design and test, FAA certification, and service in the air. It performed well and had no major problems during its creation and evolution. I performed my job well but didn't really get noticed for doing anything spectacular.

I noticed a few engineers were getting attention from the higher levels. These were the engineers who tackled a problem and helped solve it. Ironically, some of the problems being solved were actually created by the very people who were solving them. No one seemed to notice that some of these stars created the problems. Management was too busy lauding them for finding solutions.

If a business has a problem, it is costing the business money. The longer the problem persists, the more costly it becomes. When it is solved, the person who solved it is a hero, a star.

Needless to say, I am not recommending that you create a problem so you can solve it and become a hero. But I do recommend that you look around and see what problems do exist in your organization. When you find one, think about what you would do to solve it. If you are confident that you can contribute to the solution then ask if you can work on the problem.

In solving a problem, you must identify the root cause of the problem, not the symptoms. For instance, if the hallway is filling with smoke, there is a fire somewhere. To get a large fan to clear the hallway of the smoke is treating the symptom of the problem. The root cause of the problem is the fire. Until you find the fire, put it out, determine what caused it and fix that cause, you are blowing smoke and not solving the problem.

Some people do not devote the necessary effort to determining the root cause. They latch on to a symptom and solve that. They are then bewildered when the problem persists.

You must spend the time determining the true root cause of the problem. Once you successfully do that, you are in a position to solve the problem and maybe becoming a hero.

If you don't become a hero, you will become a resource person. This is a person who management turns to for their thoughts on a variety of problems facing the business. Resource people are valuable to the business and are usually compensated accordingly.

When a problem persists, management will gladly accept your help if you volunteer it. On more than one occasion, I have become aware of problems in one of our businesses. If I think I can help solve a problem I ask if I can work on the problem. I can't remember one instance in which management didn't let me participate once I had volunteered.

Don't be shy or bashful. If you see a problem, think of what you might do to solve it. Step up to the bar, volunteer your services, solve the problem and enjoy a more meaningful career.

Lesson 12

DON'T BELIEVE EVERYTHING YOU ARE TOLD

I led a course in program management at GE for a number of years. It had been put together by my company and was, in my opinion, a very good course.

A few days were spent on learning the theory and basics of program management. We discussed the details of defining, planning, and executing programs. The next day, I divided the class into four teams and unveiled four Revell plastic kits of a workable V-8 automobile engine. I don't know if they still make the kit; however, it contained many parts and took some time to build. When complete, you could put a battery in the model and the pistons moved up and down as in a real engine.

The purpose of introducing the kit was for the teams to each put together a program plan with timelines for building the kit. Each task was defined in the instructions. Not identified was the time it took to perform each task and whether different tasks could be done in parallel. The teams had to figure out those details and put them in to their program plan.

I announced that on the day before the plans were completed, we would convene and each team would follow their plan and build the engine kit.

I further announced that we would have a little fun by making the exercise into a competition. The team that assembled the engine first and demonstrated that it ran would win and would get a small prize. I also mentioned that the record for building the engine was fifty-nine minutes.

The teams worked laboriously on putting together their schedules. There was a lot of discussion and give and take regarding the timing of each task; how long it would take the glue to dry, how much they could accelerate that time if they brought in a hair dryer, how they could do two things at the same time, and so on.

When they had their program plans together they submitted them for my review. It was amazing that all of the plans came in at times of around fifty-nine minutes. Some were a few minutes shorter and some were a few minutes longer. All were in that general ballpark.

The next class started with each team enthusiastically gathered at their workstations with an unopened kit. Very quickly the teams started to fall behind in their plans, got frustrated, and started to panic. The reason was simple. All of the plastic parts were connected to trees used in the plastic molding process. All of the parts had to be removed from the trees, which took several minutes. Not one team had planned that task as part of their plan because it had not been called out in the instructions. This was an advanced model kit, not for beginners. The instructions assumed you would know to separate the parts from the trees and therefore didn't mention that task.

As the assembly continued, the teams all fell behind their schedules. The time required to assemble each component had been underestimated. I'd encourage the teams to review their critical paths to see if anything downstream might be tightened up. There wasn't another task whose time could be adjusted and each team plodded along knowing they were going to miss their schedules.

The average for each team to assemble the engines was usually more than two hours. This was more than double the time each had estimated.

When all engines were built, I would launch discussions pertaining to what was learned. The topics I would prod were well defined and one of them was a discussion of the schedule. Why did it take so much longer to build the kit than the plan called for? The answer usually was that we underestimated the complexity of the model and just how long it would take to build it.

That led to another series of questions. How is it that all teams grossly underestimated the schedule by a factor of two? Why did all the teams have similar estimates around fifty-nine minutes? Invariably the answers were that since the record was fifty-nine minutes, each team had enough confidence that they could meet or beat the record. They knew going into the planning that their schedules would end up in the one hour time frame.

Tilt! A lesson is to be learned here. You can't go into a planning session with a pre-determined time schedule. When you do the planning, you let the plan tell you how long the project will take. If there is a time requirement placed by management or the needs of the business, and your plan is longer, you must examine the plan to see what tasks can be modified or deleted to shorten the time. To decide the timing before doing the planning begs for a disaster. In our class, the disaster was that each team was over an hour late.

That was a tilt. Here comes a whammy. After that discussion I would state, in the most serious face I could muster, "Oh by the way, you need to know that I lied to you about the record. No team has ever come close to building the model in fifty-nine minutes. I made that up. Most teams take about two hours."

I would only have to wait a second or two for some pretty indignant questions about why I lied. I would explain that I estimated the kit would take three hours to build. If I led the teams to believe it could be built in one hour, they'd probably cut an hour off the original estimate and accomplish the task in two hours. I was right because I observed that each team worked a lot harder when they got behind the schedule.

I would continue the discussion that in real business situations I would never lie to anyone in order to motivate them. I can think of a multitude of ways to motivate people without telling a lie or misleading them. However, not all managers are alike. Over the course of their careers they will encounter some who don't tell the truth or are misleading for one purpose or another. You can not believe everything that you are told.

When someone tells you something, the first thing you must do is apply some sort of a sanity check to it. Ask yourself if it makes sense. If it doesn't make sense, ask the person for some more information. Ask for details. Challenge the person until it does make sense.

Remember this saying, "In God we trust. All others will be required to provide data."

Lesson 13

DON'T ANSWER THAT QUESTION

Have you ever been asked by your manager to give your opinion of the performance of a peer? I have reformed and no longer answer those questions.

I remember a manager for whom I worked a number of years ago. I was a resource person at the time, someone people sought for advice. From time to time my manager would ask me what I thought about various people. I was younger then and answered the questions as honestly as I could. I was proud of being a resource person, got many questions from many people, and answered all to the best of my ability. In retrospect, answering those questions about my thoughts of colleagues may have been one of the dumbest things I have done during my career.

In two cases, the people I was asked about were actually not "the brightest bulbs in the chandelier". Neither was doing a good job in my opinion and in the opinions of others in the organization. I gave the manager my honest opinions which I felt were accurate assessments. In each of these two cases the manager thanked me for my opinions but also told me he was surprised with my assessments.

He was surprised with my assessment because he had asked others the same question and all had responded positively about the two individuals. They did not give honest assessments because they knew the manager really liked the two individuals. They told him what he wanted to hear and they were smart enough to know he didn't want to hear the truth.

Months later, one of the two became pregnant and left the organization. The other got a great promotion. And I decided I wasn't going to answer those types of questions ever again.

I recommend that you don't answer those questions either.

I saw someone who handled these questions in a different manner. When the manager asked him what he thought about a particular person, he would turn the tables by asking the manager what he thought about the person. When the manager finished with his assessment, my friend would simply tell the manager, "I agree with you".

There are various ways to beg off answering the question. You can say that you are not comfortable appraising the performance of peers and just don't do it. You can say that you haven't really thought much about your peer's performance and therefore aren't in a position to give an opinion.

Whatever you do, don't answer the question. You have nothing to gain by answering it and everything to lose.

Lesson 14

THE 15-SECOND ELEVATOR RIDE

A general manager once asked me to tell him what I would tell Jack Welch if I found myself alone with him for only a few seconds. I thought for a while and the GM said, "Times up, Jack just left the building." The point was well taken, but he continued with the lesson.

He explained that if you were riding an elevator by yourself, the door opened and Jack Welch entered, and you were alone with him for 15 seconds, you would do one of three things. The first was that you would be stunned and say nothing. The second was that you would say something about the weather or last night's baseball game. The third was that you would say something intelligent or ask a great question. The latter would be so good that Jack would be impressed and want to spend a little more time with you.

If you hope to make the 15-second meeting to be meaningful you need to think about your statement or question now. You need to figure out what it will be and keep it at the front of your brain. The world will change, so your statement will need to be changed from time to time because you never know when Jack will jump on that elevator.

Is there a leader in your business with whom you'd love to have a 15-second encounter? Is there a chance that you might run into this leader in an elevator, in a hallway, or in a local restaurant? If so, do you have your 15-second statement or question ready? Is it so good that the leader will want the discussion to go beyond 15 seconds?

You may wonder if this exercise is worthwhile. Will you ever have a chance encounter with the leader? I can not answer that question. Jack never jumped on my elevator but I was ready for him if he ever did.

Lesson 15

TOOT YOUR OWN HORN

One of my managers told me long ago that I needed to toot my own horn because I couldn't count on someone else tooting it for me. I was a young engineer and was putting 200% effort into everything I did. My manager told me that there would be times when I was doing something special or working extraordinarily hard and I would not get credit for the effort because no one was aware of what I was doing.

It almost goes without saying that if you accept this advice you must figure a way to toot your horn in a manner that isn't arrogant or braggadocio. There are ways to accomplish the mission. For instance, if you had to work all weekend on an assignment in order to finish it by Monday, there is nothing wrong with letting your boss know that fact. The conversation can be as simple as saying, "I've completed this assignment and had no idea how difficult it would be. I probably put in twenty hours over the weekend to get it done". Don't dwell on the effort any more than that. You've delivered the message and to belabor it would have no benefit.

I have found it to be relatively easy to let key people know how hard I was working and what I was accomplishing in a simple sentence or two. In doing so I don't think I've ever come across as arrogant. I also know that, had I not thrown in a little statement about what I had done, no one would be aware of my efforts and accomplishments.

I know this lesson has benefited me. During performance appraisals I sometimes hear back exactly what I had told my manager when I tooted my horn.

The best horn tooting story I ever heard involved Gerhard Neumann, the retired Group Executive of GE's Aircraft Engine Group. Gerhard was a legend in his own time and many stories circulated about his adventures and career. I heard them from too many people who knew him for the stories not to be true.

Gerhard was a mechanic for the Flying Tigers during World War II. He had to repair engines while they were still hot in order to get the planes back into combat as quickly as possible. His hands were scarred from burns he suffered because a lot of replacement parts were hard to reach. When he became the leader of the Aircraft Engine Group, he insisted that we design engines so that they could easily be maintained. I don't know anyone who wouldn't follow his advice and would pity the poor person who didn't follow it.

I can not attest to this story; however, I heard it from many sources during my career at GE. Gerhard was a relatively young engineer and came to GE to complete an application for employment. The clerk in the reception area took his application and told him someone would get back to him in a week or two.

Gerhard noticed that there were phones and phone directories in the reception area so you could call the person you were visiting to let them know you had arrived. Gerhard asked the receptionist for the name of the person who was in charge of the business. When he got the person's name, he looked up the extension in the phone directory and called the number.

As luck would have it, the executive's secretary was not at her desk and the executive answered the telephone. This was good because Gerhard wanted to talk to the executive and not his secretary anyway.

Gerhard introduced himself and told the executive that he had just completed an employment application which was going to take GE a week or two to review. He told the executive that, if it took that long, there was a very good chance that GE would lose an opportunity to hire one of the best aircraft engineers in the country. Gerhard was going to complete an employment application at GE's competitor and there was a good possibility he would not be available in a few weeks. Gerhard closed the conversation with a statement that he would rather work for GE and that GE would be very disappointed some day in the future when they realized that they had let one of the best engineers in the country get away to their competition.

As the story goes, the executive invited Gerhard to lunch and hired him sometime during the meal. Years later, Gerhard replaced the executive as the leader of the Aircraft Engine Group.

I believe this story because I heard it from many different people who were around when Gerhard joined GE. I also believe it because I worked under Gerhard's leadership and can tell you that he was a colorful, dynamic leader.

The moral of the story is the lesson I learned as a young engineer. Toot your own horn because you can't count on someone else to toot it for you.

Lesson 16

NETWORK, NETWORK, NETWORK

I had the good fortune to work for GE for twenty-five years. GE is well-known for many reasons, two of which are the caliber of its people and the quality of its training programs. I can attest to both.

During the last half of the 1980's I worked closely with many people in GE Lighting who later left GE and advanced to responsible positions of leadership in other businesses.

Bob Nardelli became CEO of Home Depot. Stephen Rabinowitz became CEO of General Cable. Jack Irving became an Executive VP for Lockheed-Martin. Fred Grunewald became President of Overhead Door Corporation. Mike Butler became President of Char-Broil. Dan Hebert became President of the Leggett and Platt Aluminum Group. Marty Dorio became President of Clark Equipment. Harry Franze became President of AMF Bakery Systems, a division of AMF.

I have not listed these people to brag or to "name-drop". If that were my intent, I would list all 125 people that I worked with at GE Lighting who advanced to responsible positions as CEO's, presidents, and vice-presidents in other businesses. I admit that I am proud to know them and to have worked with them; however, I list them to give some real examples of people who comprise my "network".

Before I discuss networks, I need to let you know how times have changed since I entered the workforce. When I graduated from college, job offers were more plentiful than they are today. One evaluated job offers carefully before choosing one because of the culture in those days. Generally speaking you chose a company for a lifetime. You joined a company with the intent of retiring from that same company many years later. Loyalty was a hallmark of American business and its employees returned the same loyalty.

With the huge growth of competitive pressures and the true globalization of business during the last quarter-century came tremendous cost-cutting pressures. Layoffs, plant closings, and business failures became commonplace and the business/employee loyalty became a victim. Today, young people entering the workforce can expect to work for several companies before retiring.

The commercial aircraft industry provides an excellent example of what happened. In 1960, aviation had been around only fifty-seven years. Jet powered commercial aviation was only in its first decade! All commercial aircraft, with the exception of that behind the Iron Curtain, was developed and manufactured in the United States. Jet engines for those planes came from GE or Pratt & Whitney.

Twenty years later, jet engines were being built by Rolls Royce in England and SNECMA in France. The Airbus was being built by Aerospatiale in France. If you wanted to buy a super-sonic transport, you had to buy it in Europe. Today when you fly on a commuter jet, there's a good chance it was made in Canada or Brazil.

The emergence of new, global competitors turned the American aviation industry on its ear. Aircraft and engine companies had to layoff thousands of employees to remain competitive. Many aircraft companies merged with others to also stay competitive, giving rise to even more downsizing.

When the increased competitive pressures landed, the employment-for-life culture died a quick death. Thousands upon thousands of people had to look for new jobs and many didn't have a clue where to start. They didn't know where to look. They had forgotten how to write a resume. And their interviewing skills were rusty at best.

A new industry, with its own growing pains emerged – outplacement agencies. These agencies taught people how to search for employment opportunities, how to write resumes that got attention, and how to conduct strong interviews.

There were three sources of finding opportunities – advertisements of job openings, search agencies (head hunters), and friends. They discovered that the effectiveness of each was about 10%, 15%, and 75% respectively. In other words, it wasn't what you knew - it was who you knew that counted. Utilizing friends to help you find job opportunities became known as "networking".

Another avenue available today is the Internet at sites like "monster. com". I have no statistics to measure the effectiveness of these new sources of opportunities, but am willing to bet that networking remains the best source.

I have worked for three companies since leaving GE. Looking at a portion of my network, how many opportunities came from each of the sources? If you guess 100% from networking, you are correct.

You never know when you'll be looking for another job. It is, however, safe to say that there is a very high probability in today's environment that the day will come when you will be looking, voluntarily or otherwise. Given that probability, you need to consciously develop, document and nurture your network starting today.

Here's what I recommend you do:

1. Set up a spreadsheet which includes name, address, company, position, business phone, home phone, e-mail, and the date last contacted.
2. Start the list with the colleagues and managers you work with. After all, they know your capabilities best. Include as much of the information about them as you can and set out to fill in any missing blanks in your spreadsheet.
3. Add everyone with whom you've worked who has left your company for greener pastures.
4. Now turn to customers and technical societies. List the people you have encountered in the course of doing your work. Don't list everyone from a directory. Your list should include only those people you know and who know you.
5. Complete your list with neighbors and people you've worked with in your community. You'll be surprised how many people you know well from church, the soccer field, etc.
6. It is important that you stay in touch with these people, particularly, as their careers advance and they move about the country. Make an effort to contact each person on your list every six months to a year. Understand that those people are busy and don't have time to chat for an hour. However, they will be happy to hear from you and won't mind spending a few minutes catching up.
7. Greeting cards for everyone on the list over the year-end holidays are also a nice way to stay in touch. If you have the time, include a brief personalized note.
8. As people on your list move on, make sure you keep your list up to date.

When you find yourself looking for a new job and you activate your network, your conversation should be relatively simple and should involve only two questions. After calling someone and telling them that you are in the job market, tell them you have updated your resume and would they be kind enough to critique it? This gets the resume in their hands without asking them for a job and opens the door for a follow-up call to discuss your resume. Before ending the conversation, ask if they know of anyone who might be looking for someone with your skills. If they give you a name, you will have an advantage over others because you can mention the person who gave you his or her name. They can call that person for a recommendation.

Finally, never become discouraged if a phone call leads nowhere. The last time I sought new employment, I had three job offers from three people who were little help on my two previous searches. I didn't remove them from the list because they didn't help. I realized that when I called them on previous occasions, they did not need anyone with my particular skills. Besides, they were friends and friends comprise the list.

* * * *

Start your network list because you may need it someday. Keep in touch with your network because it's a good way to keep friendships alive in these busy times.

Lesson 17

S.A.R.A.

When Jack Welch took the reins of General Electric he inherited a somewhat bloated and lethargic group of businesses. To his credit, he quickly recognized what he had inherited and set a course to change it. One of the ingredients in the recipe for success was layoffs. There were many layoffs and some were of hefty magnitudes.

While Jack knew there had to be massive layoffs, he prepared the people for life after GE with the best training programs in the world. I believe he cared about the people and had compassion for them. He understood these events were not easy for both the affected people and the managers and he did whatever he could to make these as painless as possible.

The layoff lists were prepared with exacting care through a series of forced rankings based on objective parameters. The rankings were done by more than one person in order to eliminate any possibility of favoritism.

If you were a manager who had to inform someone of a layoff and there were a number of layoffs to occur, you found yourself attending a compulsory meeting the night before. You had to go through training conducted by three or four psychologists. The training taught you how to have the discussion in a professional, but compassionate, way.

The psychologists told us how the people would feel and how we would feel. They told us that they would be available for a period after the layoffs to counsel anyone who felt the need to talk to someone. I know of no other company that goes to such lengths to help people affected by a layoff.

They told us that people would go through a series of emotions and coined the acronym S.A.R.A which stood for shock, anger, rationalization, and acceptance. These emotions would probably overlap each other but they would occur in that order.

For this example we will use a fictitious person named Fred.

Shock – When Fred is informed he will probably be shocked. He has worked hard for the company, has received good performance appraisals, and honestly didn't expect to be affected by the layoffs.

Anger – Shock gives way to anger pretty quickly. If he's not angry before he gets home, he will be shortly afterwards. Fred's spouse will probably remind him of the kids' soccer games he missed because he had to work late. There may be other sacrifices they made as a result of Fred's dedication to the company. Fred's wife will remind him of all the sacrifices and may even let him know how dumb he has been. She's in shock and angry as well.

Rationalization – At some point down the road, Fred will be able to rationalize his situation. He may conclude that his boss was the dumb one for letting him go. He may conclude that the company will soon be in dire straights for letting so many good people go. Whatever he rationalizes will be good because it will be the stepping stone to the last emotion.

Acceptance – After Fred rationalizes his situation, he can accept it. It's done and he can do nothing about it. He accepts it and gets on with the business of starting a new phase in his life.

The importance of understanding S.A.R.A. is that until Fred works his way through the series of emotions and gets to the acceptance stage, Fred can not help himself. The various emotions affect him and impact his ability to get on with life. It is important for managers and others dealing with Fred to know what he's going through, understand why he is not himself, and not let that get in the way of helping him.

S.A.R.A is even more important to understand if you are involved in other negative work situations, such as a plant closing. Federal law requires that people be informed of the plant closing at least sixty days prior to it happening. These people will be remaining on the job for a while and will be dealing with their emotions while working. You must help each one of them get to the acceptance phase as soon as possible in order to have them be productive.

I also believe that people can go through S.A.R.A. as a result of non-job related events. Sudden loss of a loved one is a perfect example. There can be shock, anger, rationalization, and then acceptance. When that happens to someone working with you, you need to understand their emotions and pro-actively try to help them through the emotions and get to the acceptance phase as soon as possible.

Finally understand that someday something could happen to you which could result in your experiencing S.A.R.A. It happened to me and my awareness of S.A.R.A. helped me become whole over a short weekend.

I was hired as the general manager of a wholesale bakery with responsibility for the profit and loss of the business. Mine was one of seven bakeries under the parent company.

It was a family owned business and had been run for decades in an autocratic fashion. I was hired because the owner had read an article stating that an empowered environment would get better results. I understood empowerment and quickly got the job.

A bakery is a challenging business. Your orders for the day (and production demand) come in on the fax machine the night before.

Because of the shelf life of the product, there is no way to build any inventory. On some days, the demand exceeds your capacity.

When demand exceeds capacity, you quickly call a sister bakery in the organization to see if they can ship a load of product to you that day.

One day while I was at an off-site meeting, I got a call from Judy, our production manager. She told me we had high orders for that day and she needed to order a load from one of the other bakeries. I think my response was, "and?" She explained that my predecessor required her to get permission before ordering a load from another bakery. I told her that I expected her to make that decision herself and to let me know whenever she had a chance at a later time. She was empowered.

Not an hour passed and I got a call from the VP of Operations at home office. He couldn't believe that I hadn't called him to let him know we were buying a load and he was flabbergasted that I would let Judy make that decision.

I guess at that point I knew I was in trouble. The company thought they wanted empowerment in the organization, didn't have a clue what it was, and went ballistic when it happened.

Eight months later our sales had increased 11% and our net profit increased 43%. Also, eight months later on a Friday afternoon I was fired because, "they didn't like my style".

I got through S.A.R.A. over the weekend and started my networking phone calls on Monday morning, void of any troubling emotions. I'm sure my understanding of S.A.R.A. helped immensely.

<u>Lesson 18</u>

EVERYONE ON EARTH HAS A PURPOSE

Without getting deeply philosophical or religious, I believe that each of us on earth has been given life for a purpose. I believe many people, like me, wonder at some time during their lives why they are here. We wonder about the purpose of our lives.

Christopher Columbus was here to discover a new world. George Washington was here to found and lead a great nation. Thomas Edison was here to invent a number of things which impact our lives. Dr. Albert Sabin was here to discover a vaccine to prevent a debilitating disease.

For most of the rest of us finding the answer to why we are here is not so easy. That doesn't stop many of us from wondering about the answer.

One day I was in someone's office and saw a framed saying on the wall. It stated that:

"EVERYONE ON EARTH HAS A PURPOSE. SOME ARE HERE TO SERVE AS BAD EXAMPLES."

I laughed when I read the statement but thought about it long after. When I got past the laughter I realized that it was so true.

We have all witnessed and been effected by people who have set bad examples in our careers. If we can persevere from their behavior, we can learn so much from them. We can learn what not to do as we go forward.

Have you met the fellow who takes your work and presents it as his own? I've met more than one of them, didn't like them, and learned to always give credit where it was due.

Have you met the manager who yells, screams, and loses his temper frequently? I have and I learned from them to treat all people with dignity and respect.

Have you met the person who has trouble telling the truth? I have and I've learned to be honest even when it hurts.

I've met an uncountable number of people who are serving as bad examples. I don't get angry at them because I can learn as much from them as I can from the best teachers in the world. Pay attention to them. Study them. They have much to offer.

Finally, look in the mirror. Could it be that you have some characteristic that serves as a bad example? Are you teaching people more than you realize? If so, there's time to change. You need to find another purpose for your life and you need to start today.

Lesson 19

HAVE A PLAN FOR EVERYTHING

One of my favorite sayings is, "Failing to plan … is planning to fail". For everything of significance in business that you do, you need a good plan to guide you and good execution to keep you from failing.

Let's assume you own and manage a restaurant. The day-to-day activities of the restaurant are considered to be an operation. They involve ordering food and supplies, staffing and scheduling, preparing and serving food, cleaning, and all other activities you do each day to make the restaurant a successful business. An operation is continuous and is something you repeat every day. You undoubtedly have a business plan to guide you in the operation of your restaurant. In fact, you probably shared that business plan with your bank if you borrowed money to get the restaurant started. Your business plan will include revenue and profit objectives as well as details pertaining to all aspects of your operation.

In the course of running your restaurant you will also undertake projects from time to time. Each project is unique and is performed only one time to accomplish specific objectives. Perhaps you've had discussions with your customers or even conducted surveys, and have concluded that if you opened during breakfast hours and installed a buffet table, you would grow your business appreciably. If you decide to proceed with this idea you will be performing a project and you will need to develop a project plan.

We will deal here with the development of project plans as opposed to business plans or operating plans.

The first step in developing a plan is to define the objectives of the project. These are extremely important for a number of reasons. The objectives define the end point or destination of the project. If you don't define the destination of your journey, you will never know when you arrive. Meeting the objectives means you have arrived at the project's completion and constitutes success.

Every project has three dimensions. They are performance, timing, and costs. The objectives of your project must include all three dimensions. You will define the performance objectives with a specification, the timing objectives with a schedule, and the cost objectives with a budget. The specifications, schedule, and budget become your objectives. Meeting all three will constitute success, and missing any of the three constitutes a failure.

It is important that the objectives be specific, attainable, and measurable. On the timing and cost dimensions you are dealing with weeks and dollars, both of which are easily measured. On the performance dimension it is equally important that the specification be defined in terms of measurable parameters.

When the objectives are clearly defined, they become the basis for planning the tasks to be accomplished during the project.

In our project, the objectives are fairly easily defined. The performance objective is to extend the operating hours to include breakfast service, including a buffet. You decide that you will open the restaurant at 6am once you have everything in place, and you will attract 100 customers for breakfast each day. Additionally, you have an objective of increasing the restaurant's revenue by a certain percentage. Let's set the objective at 20%. Finally, it is also an objective to accomplish this with no increase in the size of the restaurant.

For the cost objective let's assume you have a budget of $30,000 to complete the project. The timing objective is set at three months.

As you plan and execute the project, you must keep the objectives in the forefront. Again, meeting all objectives will constitute success and missing any of the objectives will constitute failure. For instance, if you complete the project on time and within budget but do not get any customers for breakfast, your project will be a failure. You'll do fine if you keep in mind throughout the project that "it isn't okay to fail".

Once the objectives have been determined, then you can turn your attention to developing a plan to meet those objectives.

A plan is a model, on paper or on a computer, of the tasks that must be performed to accomplish the objectives. Each task contains a description of the work to be performed, the time required to perform it, links to previous tasks it is dependant upon, and the costs associated with the task.

When all the tasks are defined, listed, and linked, they, along with the objectives, form the plan.

It is important for you to realize one critical point about plans. They are essentially our best estimate of future events but they are based solely upon our past experiences. Since we can't predict future events infallibly, the probability of all the tasks happening as we visualize them will be close to zero. In other words, it is highly probable that the plan will not unfold as we predict and hope for. We must set up procedures as we execute the plan to rapidly identify the variances which are certain to occur.

Why put the effort into developing a plan if it won't happen as we predict? Think of the plan as a roadmap leading to a final destination.

As we start our journey along the road something will happen that gets us off course. With a good plan and procedures to check progress against the plan, we will be able to quickly identify when we deviate. The sooner we identify a deviation, the easier it is to correct the direction and get back to the original roadmap. The longer it takes to identify a variance, the more difficult it will be to correct the problem.

Plans are also an excellent way to communicate with everyone involved in the project. Each member of the team should have a copy of the plan and will be able to determine his or her contribution to making the plan successful.

After the objectives are defined, all members of the project team should gather to put together a list of all tasks and the timing and costs required to perform each task. These estimates must come from the people who will be doing the work. They are the people who best know the details of what must be done, and are thus the best people to estimate the time and costs. Additionally, by involving the people who will be doing the work, you are giving each individual a degree of ownership in the plan. If they "own" the plan, they will do a better job of performing to the plan.

While our restaurant project is fairly simple, we will have to assemble a team to make it happen. We will need a carpenter to design and build the buffet table. We will need the head cook to train the other cooks in preparing breakfast foods. We've decided that breakfast will include the buffet but we will also offer food from a menu. We will need our local printer to design and print our breakfast menus. We will need to add additional waitresses and will work with a local employment agency. Finally, we will need to advertise our new hours of extended operation so we should have our ad agency representative involved. All of these people will comprise our team and must participate in the planning exercise.

The next step is to have a meeting with the team and develop a list of the tasks which each must accomplish to meet our objectives. Keep in mind as you develop the plan you are predicting the future. Since none of us have the ability to do that infallibly, it is important that you include a few dummy tasks, with time and dollars, to provide a contingency when things do go astray.

After you launch the plan, you will want to check progress frequently. Again, the sooner you identify a variance, the easier it is to correct. For that reason, you will want to break down some lengthy tasks into sub-tasks of a few weeks each.

After you have determined all the activities necessary to perform the project, the next step is to determine the dependencies. In many cases, some tasks must be completed before other tasks can be started. In the restaurant project, you must decide what breakfast items will be offered before you can design a menu. You must design the menu before you can print it. Understanding the dependencies is crucial to putting together a good plan.

Once you have defined all the tasks, their dependencies, timing, and costs, you will want to get them into a chronological order and show the timing of each on a timeline. This is called a Gantt chart and can be drawn out by hand. However, if you do a number of complicated projects it is best to buy a software program to do this for you. The standard in most businesses seems to be Microsoft Project™. It will draw the Gantt chart and calculate the "critical path" for the project.

Understanding the critical path concept and knowing which tasks are critical will enhance your odds of success in your project.

Consider our restaurant project. A number of tasks can be performed simultaneously. For instance, the buffet table can be designed and built at the same time the menu is being designed and printed. Both must be done before ads are printed and new hours and breakfast service start. Suppose the path containing the buffet table is eight weeks long and the parallel path containing the menu is only six weeks long. The buffet table path is the longest in the project and becomes the critical path. If anything along the critical path slips, the entire project will slip by the same amount of time. This is the path you must manage very closely.

The menu path is parallel to the critical path and is two weeks shorter. But it is not on the critical path. The menu task can slip as much as two weeks and won't impact the overall timing of the project. We refer to these two weeks, the difference between the buffet table timing and the menu timing, as slack time.

The concept of the critical path helps you focus your attention on the tasks which will impact the ultimate timing. Non-critical tasks can slip by an amount equal to their slack and the project can still finish on time.

This is where software becomes important. I have managed projects with as many as a hundred distinct paths but only one critical path. Determining it by hand would have been quite tedious; however, with good project management software, the critical path can be determined with one keystroke.

After your plan is completed you need to review the timing and the cost estimates. As we developed the plan, we placed no constraints upon each of the contributors. Now that the plan is complete we may find that it runs a few weeks longer than our objective or costs a few dollars more than our budget. If so, we must look for opportunities to cut time or costs from some of our tasks. When we find them, it will be necessary to revise the plan and check to see if we now have a different critical path.

Once you have your final plan and are satisfied it will meet the objectives of the project, you should hold a kick-off meeting with all the people who will be performing the tasks. Pass out copies of the plan and walk through the details so everyone understands what is expected and when it's expected. End the meeting with a brief discussion of "it ain't okay to fail". Your project will then be launched.

Lesson 20

NOTHING IS EVER 99% COMPLETE

Now that you have planned and launched your restaurant project, you must manage the project. To do that, you will need to have weekly meetings with the subcontractors, measure the progress against the plan, identify variances, and develop alternatives to correct the variances. Each of these will be discussed, but first I want to point out something important about progress measurements.

You will recall that designing and building the buffet table was a task that was predicted to take eight weeks. Also, it was on the critical path which meant that any slip would result in a slip to the entire project.

When conducting weekly progress meetings, the following scenario is not too far-fetched. At the end of the second week, the carpenter will tell you he is 25% complete and is on schedule. At the end of four weeks he will be at 50% and at the end of six weeks he will be at 75%. At the end of eight weeks, when he should be 100% complete, he tells you he is almost done and is at 99% completion. The problem is that the building supply company has back-ordered the molding. All other local suppliers are also out of molding. The good news is that when it comes in, it will only take a few hours to complete the buffet table.

This is an absolute disaster because the local Board of Health will not allow the operation of a buffet table for sanitary reasons if molding is not installed. The project's completion date will slip by the number of days it takes the building supply company to get the molding.

Since the slip was discovered at the end of the project there is no time left to recover. The project will fail in the time dimension and the incremental revenue from breakfast service will be delayed until the molding arrives.

This problem could have easily been averted in the planning stage. The eight week buffet table task should have been broken down into subtasks, each of which would be about a week long. One of those subtasks should have been to "order and receive the molding". It could have been done early in the project.

If the tasks and subtasks are all about one week long, then the progress on the week it was due would either be 0% or 100%. The molding problem would have surfaced early in the project and alternatives, such as searching for molding in another city or state, could have been explored. However, you didn't plan the project in enough detail and the problem didn't surface until it was too late.

The secret is that you never allow a task or subtask to be partially complete. It is either 100% complete or it isn't complete. You never allow anything to be in between. You never allow anything to be 99%.

The key to completing the plan successfully lies in your weekly progress reviews. Involve all of the contractors in the meeting. They will have numerous ideas and broad experiences and can be quite helpful when you need to solve problems.

Also keep in mind that the main reason for conducting weekly progress meetings is to uncover problems. Look for problems. Solicit problems. Remember that the sooner you identify problems, the easier they are to solve.

<u>Lesson 21</u>

RECOVER OR RE-PLAN

In the previous chapter we discovered that the molding for the buffet table wasn't available. We discovered this fact near the end of the project and determined that, since the buffet table was on the critical path, the project would slip and miss the planned completion date. We also learned that, had we planned the project a little better, this problem would have been identified much earlier.

Had we been able to identify the problem earlier, we would have brainstormed alternatives to "recover" and not impact the final date. Some recovery options would be to; (1) conduct a national search for the molding, and; (2) substitute different materials for the molding. One of these alternatives might have been possible within our time requirements and would have constituted our recovery plan.

Since the problem wasn't identified in time to "recover", we must now brainstorm alternatives; however, we must issue a new plan reflecting the revised finish dates. In addition to the previous two options we identified for recovery which remain as viable alternatives, we have a third option which would be to wait until the original molding became available. Regardless of which alternative we select, we must "re-plan" the project and issue a revised program plan so everyone knows what the new plan is.

In program management, when unplanned events happen which negatively impact the project; we call them "revolting developments". They can occur in any number of forms. The customer can change the scope of the program. Resources, such as people or supplies, can become unavailable to the project. Prices may increase substantially beyond our initial estimates. Components that are designed and built may not work. All of these are revolting developments and must be addressed.

When planning a project, it is wise to build in contingencies. Plan a little time and a little money into a dummy task and call it contingency. There is no recommended amount of time or money for contingencies. Estimate whatever you feel is appropriate to cover an unforeseen revolting development. It is imperative that you do this because you can be certain that something will surprise you as you execute the project. If its impact falls within your contingency, you will be very happy that you had the foresight to plan for it.

Even with the best planning, you will someday have a revolting development in one of your projects that can't be addressed with your contingency account. You will then have to re-plan the project. The best way to do that is to gather the key team members and brainstorm alternatives.

For your brainstorming session, the first order of business is to state the problem and identify its root cause. Next would be to identify options that will solve the root cause and assess what each option will cost in terms of added time and costs. Finally, select an option and revise the plan.

Usually, when you re-plan, one of the dimensions of the project will be compromised. The revised plan may take more time, cost more money, or have the performance objectives lessened.

I love teaching program management and asking the students which one of a project's dimensions (cost, time, or performance) can be most easily compromised? Which of the three dimensions are the easiest to modify?

After some lively discussions I announce that the correct answer is, "it depends". It depends on a number of factors unique to your project. If you work for NASA and plan to launch a rocket with fifty experiments on board and you have a tight launch widow, the timing dimension is most critical. If you can only have forty-seven experiments ready by launch time, you forget the last three in order to meet the launch window.

If you are working on a government contract and have been told that you can not exceed the budget under any circumstances, you would probably compromise the schedule when a revolting development occurred.

In summary, you only re-plan a program when there are no other alternatives for recovery. Your best chances for recovery when a revolting development happens is to have a reasonable contingency built into the plan.

Lesson 22

POSTMORTEMS

Suppose you have just completed a major new project. Maybe you opened a new branch, closed an existing plant, completed a major acquisition, or introduced a new product. Maybe you designed and launched a new national ad campaign. Perhaps the project went as well as you expected. Possibly it went far better than you expected or it didn't go as well as you planned.

Whatever the project was and whatever the outcome, the key members of your team went through a tremendous learning experience. Since it wasn't part of their day-to-day activities, everyone was having new experiences and learning from them. The next time you do a similar project these leanings will be invaluable. Or will they?

Key members of your team may not be available the next time you do a similar project. They may have been promoted to another division or they may have left your company for a better opportunity. You need to capture the lessons learned now so you will benefit from them if you do a similar project in the future. You can capture that information by having a postmortem meeting.

Postmortem meetings should be held as soon as possible after the completion of a project while the information and experiences are relatively fresh. The key members of the team should be invited to participate even if they are not located at the headquarters operation. The travel expenses are insignificant relative to the value of the information you will capture. Someone not associated with the project should attend to take minutes. You might invite someone from human resources to facilitate the meeting.

Postmortem meetings have some rules which need to be announced at the start and need to be understood by everyone participating.

1. The meeting is being held to capture the lessons learned from doing the project. It is not being held to determine who performed well and who didn't. Therefore, personalities are not to be discussed.
2. No item can be considered as being wrong. There may be legitimate differences of opinion regarding aspects of the project. One person may feel an activity took too long while another person felt it could not have been completed more quickly. Both points of view should be discussed and both points of view should be included in the final report.
3. Do not publish an agenda for the meeting. You will have an agenda but it will not be shared in advance because you don't want "prepared" answers from participants. You want a free flowing thought process during the meeting.
4. There is no set time for this meeting. Start it early in the morning and continue it as long as necessary to get all of the information that you can.
5. Everyone is expected to participate. Put a group together and some will be quiet throughout the meeting. If you notice that someone is not participating, ask that person a question directly to force his or her participation.

The format for the meeting will be a series of questions for everyone that you prepare beforehand. The intent of the questions will be to create a lively discussion and to get as much information as possible. The following are suggested:

1. What was the objective of our project?
2. What were the results of our project? Did we meet the performance objectives? Did we meet the timing and cost objectives? If we didn't meet all the objectives, why didn't we?
3. Did we do an adequate job of planning the project? Could we or should we have done anything differently during the planning stages? What would you do differently the next time we put together a plan for a similar project?
4. Did we have the right team of people with the right mix of skills to perform a project of this nature? Did we assign enough people to the project? Did we have too many people on this project?
5. In performing the project, what did we do well? What phases of the project went better than expected? Why did they go well?
6. In performing the project, what didn't we do well? What factors contributed to this?
7. If you could do the project over again, what would you do differently?
8. What did you learn in performing this project?
9. Should we do similar projects in the future?

This list of agenda questions is not all inclusive. It is offered to show the type of information you are trying to capture. If you think of additional questions that will encourage the team members to open up and share their experiences, thoughts, and recommendations, then add to the list.

After the meeting, you need to consolidate all the information into a "White Paper". This is not a trivial task but it is necessary if you are to benefit from your postmortem in the future.

Publish the White Paper and give a copy to each team member for their files. Establish a postmortem section in your files and file your White Paper and the project plan in that section.

The next time you have a project to do, check the files to see if you have a White Paper for a similar project. If you do, I guarantee that your new project will go a lot more smoothly than the prior project.

Lesson 23

DON'T MANAGE ... LEAD

"If you are not the lead dog in the pack, the scenery never changes." Author unknown.

I have never liked the title of "manager". To me, a manager gives orders and spends the rest of his time checking timecards to make sure everyone worked forty hours in the week. If an organization is comprised of motivated and committed people, they really don't need a manager. They need a leader.

A manager exercises his authority in running his organization. Leaders use influence in running their organization. They don't give orders to subordinates, but instead inspire their team to higher levels of motivation and performance.

The first thing a leader does is to create a vision of where the business will be in the future and what it will look like. This vision includes a timing dimension when the vision will become a reality.

Leaders tirelessly communicate the vision to their team at every opportunity. They articulate the vision to the point where their team comes to "see' the vision, believes in it, and wants it to happen as much as the leader does.

Leadership is much more than creating and articulating a vision. A leader is not born a leader. A person evolves into becoming a leader by first gaining knowledge and experience and developing leadership skills.

A leader views his organization as a team. The members are not subordinates, but are considered teammates. The leader develops his skills in treating the people as members of the team. A leader considers himself as a part of the team. A leader preaches that, "We will all succeed together. There will be no heroes and there will be no losers. We will all win the game together…and we will win".

Leaders involve the team in making decisions. They can do this comfortably because they have taken the time to make sure the team is well-informed. They know the vision, the strategy, where the business is going and how it is going to get there. Everyone on the team has this knowledge, not just a selected few. A leader empowers his team. Members are empowered to make decisions which they know are right without seeking concurrence. They are empowered to do their jobs unencumbered by constant direction or orders from a manager.

It sounds simple, doesn't it? All you have to do is see a mountain you think your business needs to climb. Create a vision of that mountain and articulate it to the team. Point the direction and inspire the team to follow you to the top.

The vision part may not be difficult, but the inspiration part may present a challenge. How do you inspire the team to follow you? That's where skills and knowledge enter the equation. That's why people are not born as leaders, but have to develop knowledge and leadership skills over time.

In order for people to be inspired to follow you, they must respect you on several levels.

They must respect your knowledge. They must have confidence that you possess the technical knowledge to accomplish the task and that you will share that knowledge with them. If they don't think you have the knowledge required to climb that mountain, they will be reluctant to follow you. For that reason, true leaders never stop learning. They constantly seek opportunities to build on their knowledge base.

They also must respect your people skills. They must have confidence in your ability to motivate people. They must respect your ability to communicate effectively, to be fair to everyone, and to resolve inevitable conflicts professionally.

They must respect your value system. They have to know that you have values, character, and integrity.

Finally, you must be savvy in the ways to motivate people by your influence as opposed to your authority. There are nine recognized influence factors and techniques. I believe that four of them work far better than the others and will discuss just those four:

1. Expertise. The team members believe that you have special knowledge and are confident that they will learn some of that special knowledge if they participate in the voyage to achieve the vision.
2. Excitement. The team members feel that the voyage will be challenging and exciting and want to share in the excitement.
3. Advancement. The team members believe that the voyage to the vision will have high visibility and attainment of the vision will have significant benefits to the business. As a member of the team, the possibility of career advancement will be enhanced.
4. Friendship. The team members like the leader as well as respect him. They want the leader to succeed and want to do a good job in order to help the leader succeed.

One of the best ways to develop leadership skills is in the area of project management. If you are lucky enough to be appointed to manage a project, you will find yourself in charge of a team of people assembled to perform a project. The team members may come from sales, engineering, manufacturing, and finance departments. Chances are that no one on the team will work for you in the business organization. Thus you can't manage by authority because you can't discipline anyone on the team. You have no choice but to manage by influence. You must become a leader and you must figure out how to do that in short order.

If a project is on the horizon, try volunteering to lead that project.

In your career, you don't want to manage but you do want to lead. Gain the knowledge and hone the skills necessary to be a leader. When you can lead instead of manage you will have a far better chance of success. When you enhance your odds of success, you reduce the odds of failing. Remember, it ain't okay to fail.

Lesson 24

CREATE A SECRET VISION

Whenever I have been given an assignment, the first thing I do is spend a few minutes creating a secret vision. The vision is very personal and indeed secret. I have never, until this moment, even divulged the concept of secret visions to anyone, let alone discussed the specifics of my personal visions.

The reason for secrecy is that they are always far-fetched and the odds of them ever coming true are very remote. If one ever did come true, I would be flabbergasted. They are so far fetched that if I were to share them with anyone, that person might think I was crazy.

A few years ago, I was asked to lead the day-to-day activities in closing a manufacturing plant. Fortunately, I had closed a few plants prior to this assignment and my prior experience was invaluable to my new assignment. With no prior experience, I would have encountered a very rocky road. Closing a plant is not an easy task.

You usually get the assignment after the plant closing announcement has been made. Understandably, prior to the announcement, all planning has to be done in secret by only a few executives who probably never managed a plant closing. Unfortunately, some of their assumptions are nowhere near correct and their timetable is usually unrealistic. The early stages of this plant closing were no different. For instance, I quickly discovered that the actual number of tools to be transferred was almost double that of the executives' estimate. By the time I got the project, the executives had carved the timetable in granite and my performance would be measured against an unrealistic timetable.

Plants close for a variety of reasons. In this case a major customer had moved to an off-shore manufacturer. As a result, the plant's volume was less than that needed to break-even and the plant was running inefficiently. The plan was to transfer the remaining business to our other plants, allowing us to shut down the plant that was losing money.

In order to transfer business to other plants, it is necessary to build adequate inventories of each part to allow shipment of parts to customers while tools and equipment transfer to the receiving plant. This almost always requires that the closing plant improve its operating efficiencies in order to build adequate inventories of the parts it makes.

It gets even more challenging. The employees know they could be unemployed in a few months and are actively looking for employment elsewhere. It always seems the best employees get offers quickly and, if you don't have a good plan which includes ample rewards, you will find yourself having to increase production with a dwindling work force of the more marginal people. These people are concerned that they haven't found another job yet and are angry because of what's happening. They think you are crazy to think that they are going to increase efficiencies and production all of a sudden. Keep in mind that I'm talking about both the rank and file as well as the salaried staff.

To make matters even worse you know that, at some point in time, you will have to bring in people from the receiving plant to be trained on the equipment by the very people who will be losing their jobs.

Add to the mix a hostile union and some belligerent stewards and you have the recipe for a cake that could explode at any time during the process.

Immediately my attention turned to creating a secret vision. There was plenty of time to develop the public vision. The latter would center around closing the plant successfully in the required time frame. Success would include retaining all of our current customers by making the plant closure invisible to their operations. It also would include caring about and tending to the welfare and success of every employee impacted by the closing.

But first, I needed a secret vision. It took only a few minutes to invent. I knew that other business segments of the corporation were also closing plants. My vision was that my plant closing project would go far more smoothly and far more successfully than the others being tackled. So much so that, when all were completed, the CEO would call me, ask me how I did it, and ask me to make a presentation at the next meeting of his staff.

When I created the secret vision I knew it's odds of coming true were probably less than one in a million. When the project had outstanding results and I didn't get that phone call, I knew I had pegged the odds pretty accurately. This might beg the question, "Why bother having a secret vision?"

The reason is simple. If you believe there is one chance in a million that it will come true, it will give you the motivation and the inspiration to push beyond your limits. It will provide an additional perspective to help with decision making. It will enhance the odds of success for your project.

Upon creating the vision, you turn to clarifying your objectives and your plan. With the vision you ask, "What must I do to make the vision come true? What must happen in terms of final results?" Without the vision, the answer might be to finish the project on time. With the vision, the answer is that the project must be completed ahead of schedule. For the vision to eventually happen you must hit the ball out of the park. And your goals will be "stretch" goals.

The plan you put together for the stretch goals will be ambitious, challenging, and hard to achieve. This is the plan you're not going to share with anyone else because it's based on your secret vision and objectives. Before launching the project, you will develop a more realistic plan to meet the objectives defined by management. In effect you will have two plans – one for public consumption and one based on stretch goals. You will manage the project to meet the stretch goals.

On a few occasions I have become so excited about the stretch goals that I have shared them with my management. In all cases that has been a mistake. Management believes the stretch goals can be made and pretty soon they become the expectation. If you don't make the revised, challenging expectation you can get a poor grade even though you achieved the original objectives. Don't tell your manager that you're swinging for the fences. Just go ahead and hit the home run.

Let's return to the secret vision. A vision is something you see. I always enjoy fantasizing about it. Remember that this vision was being called to headquarters to share with the senior staff the details of how I had achieved such outstanding results. It was always fun and certainly healthy to take a break each day and embellish the secret fantasy. I would picture who was invited to the meeting. I would try to determine just what I would tell them. I would picture what clothes I would wear. As the project progressed I had developed a pretty sharp vision in full Technicolor™.

Finally, I used my secret vision as a factor in decision-making. When faced with making a decision I would evaluate all the factors. Additionally, I would ask myself if the way I was leaning in making the decision would help or hinder my secret vision from coming true.

The plant closed two days ahead of schedule. More importantly, most people left in good spirits, knowing their futures were bright and feeling as if they had been treated fairly. Many had been able to find another job. Many others were heading to extended unemployment benefits and cash grants so that they could get training and education in other fields. Many thanked me personally for caring about them and respecting them over the three month period. I was extremely gratified. As time had progressed and I had embellished my secret vision I had developed another goal. It was that when the project was over, the people would go out of their way to thank me for a job well-done. That part of the vision came true.

I never got that call to brief the senior management staff. But that didn't matter because the vision of that call helped me to put together and execute a great plan. It helped me to exceed the expectations of my management.

The next time you get an assignment put together a little far-fetched secret vision and let it help you swing for the fences.

* * * *

As I started writing this book I actually had two separate secret visions. Oh, I'm sorry that I mentioned that because I can't share either vision with you.

<u>Lesson 25</u>

CREATE A REALISTIC BUSINESS VISION

A friend called me one evening. He had been promoted from the leadership of one of our businesses to the leadership of another. It was a nice promotion as his new business was approximately six times larger than his old business. He called to ask my opinion of what he needed to do to be successful in his new assignment.

I had not been intimately involved in the new business but had some idea about its future. I knew that it faced the real possibility of losing its two biggest customers over the next few years. Together they represented about 70% of his business' revenue. One customer was in the process of going out of business and the other was considering moving its business to China. The latter would take several years so there was time to develop and implement a strategy to replace the business that was going away.

I told him that his top priority was to develop a strategy addressing the void created by the business he was losing and how he was going to fill that void. He needed to create a vision of what his new business would look like five years down the road. The strategy and vision were inseparable and feed each other during the development phase. We talked quite a while that evening and I closed by recommending that he work on the strategy and vision starting with his first day on the new job. Time would pass quickly and he needed to develop that strategy and vision as soon as possible.

All businesses should develop a strategy. Many businesses get the strategy and tactics intertwined. The strategy should focus only on where you are going. The tactics focus on how you are going to get there.

In my friend's case, his strategy would start with a simple statement that the business would fill the void created by the part of the business he was losing. It would also address how they would strategically, not tactically, do that. They could do it by introducing value-added processes to their existing core business or product line. They made components for different products and sent them elsewhere to be assembled. They could add value by undertaking the assembly process. Perhaps they could add additional products to their core business by developing expertise in processing other materials, such as plastics. Perhaps they could form a joint venture with a Chinese company and leverage that partnership to increase their revenues. They needed to brainstorm the possibilities at a high level and develop their strategy.

Once the strategy and the strategic direction were formulated and determined, the details of how to make it happen would become their tactical plan. That would include the elements required to develop a new product if new products were part of the strategy. It may require changing the skill mix of their employee base to include experts in new technologies they had to pursue in going beyond their current core competencies.

In one business for which I worked we would review our strategy each year before we put together operating budgets for the next year. Some of our customers were large automotive companies with whom it can be difficult to work. The revenue from the automotive segment of our business was about 10% and the gross income was a much smaller percentage. Each year during our planning meetings we would have to make a strategic decision about whether we wanted this business. If we ever had decided to exit that segment of the business, we would have needed a detailed tactical plan addressing precisely how to go about it.

Once your business determines its strategic direction you, as the leader, must develop a vision of what your business will look like a few years down the road when the strategy becomes reality. You must be able to close your eyes and literally take a snapshot of your new business. A vision is just that. It is what you see, what you envision. Maybe your strategy called for a new value added process such as assembling the components you make into a finished product. When you close your eyes, you envision what the assembly area will look like. Maybe you can see the assembled product. Whatever you see is your vision of the future.

Your vision needs to be realistic. It needs to be in the realm of the possible. It needs to be a vision which comes true within a certain realistic time frame.

Once you have developed your strategy and your vision you need to hammer them home with your employees. You need to take every opportunity to articulate your vision. That is the work of a leader. The troops need to see that vision of where the business is going. They need to understand it. They need to believe in the vision and that it will come true.

Because when they see it and when they believe in it, they become the ones who will make it happen. Your job is to continue repeating the vision until people understand it and believe in it. That is a key component of a leader.

Lesson 26

TAKE RISKS AND SWING FOR THE FENCES

This lesson presents a dichotomy with the other lessons and with the theme of the book. By employing this lesson, there will be failures from time to time. They will be inevitable. In your mind, they will not be okay; however, you will learn from them and move on.

In baseball, when you come to the plate, laying down a bunt will probably provide you the best odds of safely getting on base. It will be the least risky shot and your chances of striking out will be low.

The shot with the most risk at the plate is to swing for the fences and try to hit a home run. If you swing for the fences, you will hit some home runs and some base hits. Unfortunately, you will also strike out some of the times.

The bunt, with its low risk, usually has little payoff. Someone has to hit you home in order for you to score a run. The home run, on the other hand, has an immediate payoff for the team.

In business, there are risk-averse people who seem pleased with getting bunts. There are others who are comfortable with calculated risk and swing for the fences when they come to bat.

If you are an individual contributor, you should take some risk and swing for the fences whenever you have an assignment or project to perform. You will have a goal. You should evaluate the goal and examine stretch goals. Can you get the task done more quickly by doing some things differently? Can you get a better payback by doing something else differently? What are the risks associated with your stretch goals? If the risks are sensible and won't jeopardize the ultimate objectives, why wouldn't you want to tackle the stretch goals, to swing for the fences?

If you are a business leader you take risks everyday. You must also take calculated risks in your major projects and your operations. You must swing for the fences for a couple of reasons.

First, if you don't swing for the fences and if you don't take risks, your business will have mediocre results at best. If you take risks, you will hit some home runs and your business results will grow from mediocre to good and even great.

Secondly, if you are willing to take risks you are establishing a culture for your company in which it's okay for your employees to also rake risks. If your people know that it's okay to swing for the fences, then some will. If you don't establish this culture you probably won't have any employees willing to take risks.

I am not suggesting that individuals and leaders become cowboys and take reckless risks. That would ensure a lot more strikeouts than home runs and would drive the business into the ground. I am suggesting that you evaluate your goals and stretch goals. There is some risk associated with anything you do and there is also some risk with your basic plans. Understand those risks and compare them to the increased risks associated with your stretch goals. If the increased risks are reasonable, then go for them. Swing for the fence. If the increased risks are substantial, then back off and look at a lessened stretch goal.

Whatever you choose, don't be the one who doesn't take risks, lays down bunts, and only gets to first base.

Whenever you go for the stretch goals, there will be times when you fail to achieve them. You must understand that if you are a leader, you must let people know that they may fail from time to time and failure will not result in demotion or termination.

Failure will not be okay to the person who fails. He or she took risks, didn't hit the stretch goal and will feel terrible that they failed.

But there will be things to learn from the failure. The mistakes made or the things that didn't go right will become part of the learning experience and won't happen the next time.

While there will be failures, there will also be home runs and victories. In the long run, the individual will be more successful than they would have been otherwise and your business results will be better as a result.

Swing for the fences and let the people in your organization know that it's okay. Encourage calculated risk taking and support those who take risks. They are the ones who will make your company more successful.

Lesson 27

BECOME FRIENDS AND THEN DO BUSINESS

For a number of years I worked for AMF Bakery Systems, a division of AMF that manufactures equipment for large wholesale bakeries throughout the world. I joined the company as vice president of engineering and later served as vice president of sales. Having no prior experience in baking, or the food industry for that matter, I experienced a steep learning curve.

Most large industries and professions have a technical society which provides research, education, the exchange of ideas, and events to bring its members together periodically for various activities. The technical society for the baking industry is the American Institute of Baking, with headquarters in Manhattan, Kansas.

One course taught by AIB is "Baking for Non-Bakers." It is a one-week course that is both informative and fun. They teach the theory of baking in the morning and set you loose in the afternoon in the kitchen to bake.

I was fortunate that one of these classes was scheduled to start shortly after I reported for duty at AMF. Thus, I found myself in Manhattan, Kansas for the second week of my new job.

The baking industry is world-wide and my class of thirty reflected that. Participants included people from Brazil, Mexico, Egypt and Jordan. I quickly learned that the Jordanians were on a mission that included more than learning how to bake bread.

For various reasons, King Hussein had decided to build a large government bakery to supply bread for the entire kingdom. The two Jordanians were from the Ministry of Supply and were attending the course to learn more about baking, but also to meet a representative from the baking equipment side of the business to assist in making the King's vision become a reality. They were there to meet one of my new competitors! The staff at AIB was quick to introduce me as another person from the equipment side of the industry and another person with whom they might want to talk.

At lunch I called the president of my company to see if we wanted to do business in Jordan. I might just as well have asked if dogs have tails, because the answer was a resounding yes.

Remember that this was my second week with my new company. I had little knowledge of the equipment we offered and no knowledge of why our equipment would have a competitive advantage over that of the other supplier talking to them. I asked the president to "overnight" all the sales brochures and literature that would be of interest to the Jordanians and that would help me become more knowledgeable as well.

As soon as the phone call ended, I started to develop a plan to win this potential business. The first task was to stall any discussions of our equipment until I got my hands on the literature I had requested and had a chance to digest it. I learned that this was the first visit to America for the Jordanians. I decided that the best stalling tactic would be to invite the visitors to do a little sightseeing and to offer them an opportunity to do some shopping for souvenirs. I quickly made arrangements to pick up a rental car and headed to the kitchen to see if I could bake a loaf of bread.

During the first break, I asked my new acquaintances if they would like to do some sightseeing and perhaps visit some stores after class. Their eyes literally lit up as they told me that they had discussed their desires to do some shopping but weren't sure how to get around in this new environment. They were quick to add, "Mr. Brian, that is so kind of you. We would very much like to visit a 'Wal-Market'." I made a mental note that if we had to drive sixty miles to Kansas City before we found a Wal-Mart, we would do exactly that. As luck would have it, Manhattan had a Wal-Mart about two miles from our motel. The only problem was that it closed at 9pm each night.

I never imagined what I had volunteered for. We shopped and shopped and shopped. We shopped Monday night, Tuesday night, and Wednesday night. On Thursday afternoon, we skipped baking and searched for a company that could package all their new-found treasures and could arrange to ship them to Jordan. It hadn't occurred to me that, as representatives of the Minister of Supply, they were actually buying a number of items with the objective of later evaluating them for potential import.

Through all the shopping and late evening dinners at McDonald's, we talked of our families, our countries, our religions, our travels, and our interests. In the process, we started developing friendships that continue to this day.

Another benefit of the shopping sprees was that they had no time to meet with my competitor. They were very gracious about this and they did take all his sales literature. They also took mine on the last day of class. They apologized to me for not having time for meaningful business discussions during the week, but quickly added, "Mr. Harry (my president) and you must come to Amman in a few weeks so that we could conduct business."

My fifth week with AMF was spent in Amman, Jordan. The experience was extraordinary and I could not do justice to Jordan in a few paragraphs. To tell of the sights I saw, the history I learned, and the gracious people I met would require another book. Suffice to say it was a wonderful experience that still provides memories to cherish. If it were possible, I would return to Jordan in a minute.

By the way, we did spend a little time on business during the week. Four months after our visit, we signed a sweat deal to equip a large, national bakery for the kingdom of Jordan. I am certain our competitor was treated with respect by my friends. I am equally certain, he never got out of the batter's box, much less to first base on the Jordanian bakery venture.

The lesson here is obvious, whenever possible, become friends first and then do business.

This advice may not be new to some people. Long before I attended the class in Manhattan, I was aware that in certain cultures, becoming friends prior to discussing business was a desirable path to take. Yet, in spite of that knowledge, my strategy didn't include anything like developing friendships.

My strategy was to "stall" until I had the knowledge to discuss business in a meaningful way. Even though we all know a number of things that will make our missions easier, we often forget to utilize some of those things. We all need to do better jobs of taking the time to bring all of our knowledge to each venture we pursue.

In utilizing the friendship advice, keep in mind that friendships do not happen instantaneously, but take time. At a minimum, try to take a few steps to start developing a friendship before rushing into business discussions.

Whenever I meet someone for the first time in his office, I quickly scan the room for "signs of interest." They can include diplomas, paintings, posters, books, pictures, small models, or anything else that doesn't pertain to the business. I will utilize one of these to start a conversation. I will very sincerely inquire about something I spot in the first few seconds.

"I see you went to Notre Dame. What did you major in?"
"I see you have an autographed baseball. Do you enjoy baseball?"
"I see you have a skiing poster. Do you ski?"
"That is a great family portrait. Three kids must keep you and your wife busy all of the time."

The beauty of these questions is that they open the door for your host to talk about his school days, his hobbies and avocations, or his family. You can bet that all are subjects that he loves to talk about and will not mind spending the first few minutes of the meeting to discuss them with you.

You are breaking the ice with your new acquaintance. You are potentially starting a relationship that could develop into a long friendship. Finally, you are enhancing the odds of a favorable outcome at the end of the meeting.

This technique is also an excellent way to start a job interview you are conducting. Something on the resume will lead to an ice-breaking question with which to start the interview. The goal in this case is not to start a friendship. It's to put the person at ease and encourage him to speak more openly with you.

* * * *

Again, make friends and then do business. Friendship is all about getting to know someone, allowing them to know you, and truly enjoying being with one and other. You will want to do things for friends and they will want to do things for you. You may never benefit by getting their business, but you will be rewarded by the benefits of friendship and that will be worth your efforts.

Lesson 28

SIX LITTLE WORDS

Business today is truly global. It would not be surprising to be conducting business in China this month, in Mexico next month, and in Europe the following month. Nor would it be surprising to remain in America and have visitors from those or other countries over a short period of time.

We learned in the previous chapter that, if time permits, you should become friends with people and then do business. All too often time constraints make it difficult to accomplish everything you desire during a visit. I have found another exercise to be very helpful in establishing a good business relationship with people from other countries is to learn a few words of their language.

For one reason or another, most Americans know only one language – English. Some of us know enough of another language to get by in the appropriate country. It is a rare American who can speak three or four languages fluently.

Are we too arrogant to learn another language? Are we too lazy to learn another language? I don't think those are the reasons; however, I honestly don't know why more of us don't learn foreign languages, particularly since many of us spend a great deal of time in other countries.

Almost everywhere we go in major cities around the world, we encounter many people who are able to converse with us in English. That makes our travels a good bit easier. However, I've always wondered how much we are resented by those people because we seem to make no attempt to learn their native languages.

Whenever I've traveled to a foreign country I have sought someone who speaks the language and I've learned at least six words in that language. The six words are "hello", "good-bye", "please", "thank you", "yes" and "no".

When I meet someone and say hello in their language, it just seems to break the ice a little better. I usually get a smile which is quickly followed by an inquiry as to whether I speak their language. I explain that I know only a few words, but if they can teach me a few more before I leave, I will be grateful. That small gesture on my part seems to go miles in helping to start a good relationship.

I have done this over and over again whenever I travel. Without a single exception, the people I have met have told me that they are pleased that I care about their language and that I want to learn more. It has contributed to getting all my meetings off on the right foot.

As you travel the world, here are a few things that I hope will help you.

Chinese (with pronunciation in parentheses):

Hello	Nin Hoa	(Nee Haw)
Good-Bye	Zai Jian	(Zigh Jen)
Please	Qing	(Ching)
Thank You	Xie Xie	(She-u She-u)
Yes	Shi	(Shhh)
No	Bu	(Boo)

	Spanish	French
Hello	hola	selui
Good morning or Good day	buenos dias	bon jour
Good evening	buenas tardes	bon soir
Good night	buenas noches	
Good bye	adios	au revoir
Please	por favor	s'il vous plait
Thanks	gracias	merci
Many thanks	muchas gracias	merci beaucoup
Yes	si	oui
No	no	non

When you travel to other countries, seek out someone who knows the native language and ask them to teach you a few words. If you can't find someone who knows the language, buy a small dictionary and look up those six little words. If you are unable to do either of these, contact the country's embassy in Washington. They will be glad to help you.

It is worth the effort. Your trip and meetings will go very well if you learn those six little words.

Lesson 29

14,000 BRAINS

Many years ago, a CEO off a major conglomerate was visiting one of his businesses for a periodic business review. As the meeting was ending, he innocently asked the leader of the business to tell him again how many employees were in that business. The answer was 14,015 people.

The CEO was silent for a minute or two and was clearly pondering the answer. No one in the room could have imagined where he was ultimately heading with his question.

Finally he said, "Since you have 14,000 people, you obviously have 14,000 brains available for use in this business. What a tremendous resource you have at your disposal. The average human brain weighs about three pounds. That means you have about 42,000 pounds of human brains in your business. That's 21 tons of human brains. That is absolutely mind boggling."

"I am curious," he continued, "how many of those 14,000 brains are you using to help you run your business? How many of those 14,000 brains do you utilize to help you solve the business problems you encounter? How many of those 14,000 brains are you utilizing to the maximum of their capacity?"

Regardless of how the executive answered the question, he wasn't utilizing those brains as best he could. He was instructed to put together a plan to maximize the benefit of those 14,000 brains.

How many of us concentrate on the total brain power in our businesses? How many of us try to utilize every brain in our business? How many of us are satisfied that the suggestion box we mounted on the wall adequately taps into the total brain power in our organization?

Very few people put ideas into the suggestion box. Most don't take the time to offer a suggestion. Many feel that no one pays attention to their suggestions anyway.

As a manager, you must be pro-active in utilizing all the brain power in your organization. Once you decide to do so, there are probably a number of ways to maximize the benefit.

One of my favorite ways to get people involved and to use their brains is to conduct meetings with every person in the organization each month. And I mean every last person in the organization.

My meetings are billed as business reviews and usually last about a half-hour. I share the previous month's business results and the challenges facing the business. For each challenge or problem I discuss I ask for ideas about how to solve the problem. Some are offered, but I never close the meetings with enough ideas. So I challenge the people to keep thinking about the issues and tell them I will walk the halls and factory floor and will stop to see if someone has come up with any additional ideas. If anyone thinks of something and sees me, grab me to discuss your thoughts. A number of people will follow up. They are happy to be involved and feel more strongly that they are part of the team as a result.

I will also carry this one step further when I conduct brainstorming sessions, strategy meetings, or problem solving meetings. They usually involve key staff members and sometimes the engineers. I have found that it does not hurt to include a few people who wouldn't normally participate in such meetings. Perhaps I will invite a secretary, an intern, and someone from the rank and file to join us. They may just have some ideas that the "experts" haven't thought about. Try it at your next meeting and you might be surprised.

I have found three groups of people whose brains are not tapped as much as they could be. You never seem to see young people, clerical, support, and factory people in strategy sessions, problem solving meetings, and other business meetings. Yet all have brains and can use those brains as well as everyone else.

Young people don't participate because they don't have many years of experience to bring to the table. Yet they have some of the sharpest brains in your organization. Are you aware that most significant inventions were invented by young people? Alexander Graham Bell was 29 when he invented the telephone. Thomas Edison was 30 when he invented the phonograph and 32 when he invented the incandescent light bulb. All three of these inventions were accomplished between 1876 and 1879. My guess is that, in today's business world, these two geniuses would not participate in strategy development meetings or problem solving meetings at the age of 30 because they wouldn't have enough experience to significantly contribute to the meetings. I believe the lack of experience is not necessarily bad because the young person doesn't yet know many things are not possible. You need some of that silly thinking in your meetings.

The next group of underutilized brains resides in the heads of clerical people and support staff such as technicians. I really don't know why this group is underutilized. I think management just feels that these people can't contribute much more than they are doing. These people understand the business far better than you think. And each has a brain or you wouldn't entrust them with the things you do. Invite them to participate in activities beyond the scope of their duties and you will be pleasantly surprised. I sat on a department staff under a general manager. His secretary attended all staff meetings and she wasn't there to take minutes. The general manager considered her an equal to the rest of his staff members and she participated fully in all of our deliberations.

My favorite group is the factory workers. Many do menial tasks, day in and day out, which don't require a great deal of brain power. I guess management doesn't think they have much brain power or they would be doing something else for a living. That way of thinking is foolish. I can't tell you about all the factory people I've known that use their brains far more after work and are highly successful in their endeavors.

I knew a mechanic who set up a silk-screen machine in his garage to decorate T-shirts with catchy sayings he made up. He literally bought the T-shirts for pennies, fixed them up, and sold them for dollars at local flea markets on the weekends. A machine operator customized hot rods in his garage in the evenings and sold one to a magazine publisher for a huge amount of money. It graced the cover of a national hot rod magazine a few months later. There are many success stories of factory workers who became entrepreneurs after work. The point is that all of these workers have brains and are highly capable of contributing to strategy sessions and problem solving meetings.

If you discuss issues with these people, challenge them to come up with ideas, and follow up getting their suggestions, you will get some good ideas. You will be starting to optimize the brain power in your business. Most importantly, the people will feel as if they are important members of the team, will have ownership in the solutions, and will work harder to make things happen in your business.

14,000 human brains or 21 tons of human brain power is a horrible resource to waste!

Lesson 30

TRY TO WORK WITH UNIONS

Your employees may or may not be represented by a union. Most businesses leaders would prefer to not have a union. If you treat your employees as human beings and follow the lessons of this book, they don't need a union to represent them. However, someone along the line may not have treated the employees fairly and they chose to unionize. You, as the leader, must deal with a union.

I have led businesses without unions as well as businesses with unions. I have dealt with the Teamsters, the Bakery, Tobacco & Confection, and the Electrical Workers Unions. Whenever I have had a union to deal with, I have tried my best to work well with them. This doesn't always work; however, in many cases, it has worked well. If you don't try to work with them, your business will suffer.

When I say, "try to work with them," I mean try to be fair, try to see their perspective, and don't enter discussions with any prejudice or pre-conceived notions. That does not mean you are not firm with them or let them push you around.

I once led a business in Philadelphia whose employees were represented by a national union. I also had a staff that was pretty anti-union. Rather than try to work with the union, the staff would literally fight them on every issue that came up.

On a personal level, I liked the business agent for the union. He was a friendly fellow trying to do a decent job. He was easy to get along with and seemed to have an open mind. On a few occasions I would invite him to lunch so we could get to know each other better.

Whenever an employee felt that something was being done that was not consistent with the contract, they could file a grievance. There were hearings on the grievance and, if the employee was not satisfied with the results, they could appeal the findings to the next step. I think I was Step 3 of the process and the last step before arbitration.

It seems that I would hear a Step 3 grievance about every other week. I learned that my staff, which heard grievances at the lower steps, had never ever ruled in favor of the employee. Not once. In their minds, the company was always right and the employees were always wrong. What a wonderful culture in which to expect profitable, efficient operations.

I couldn't wait for an opportunity to start changing that culture. As luck would have it, I didn't have to wait long.

An employee who worked in the plant had been on extended sick leave for a few months. She notified the company that her doctor had released her to return to work on Saturday. On the Friday before, she brought the medical release form to the office manager.

She reported to work on Saturday and was promptly sent home because her foreman had not seen the medical release form.

The employee filed a grievance because she had filed the proper forms with the company, had been told she could start back to work on Saturday, reported to work and was denied work. She requested that she be paid for Saturday since she was willing to work and had been told that she could work.

Her grievance was denied in the first two meetings with the company and advanced to my attention for a decision.

In the grievance meeting, the business agent presented her case. My operations manager presented her position which was to deny payment since the employee didn't work. I learned in the hearing that the root cause of the problem was that neither the medical release form nor any communication made it from the office manager's office in the front of the building to the foreman's office in the middle of the building. I concluded that the employee should not be denied work because one of my departments was incapable of communicating with another department. I agreed to pay the employee one day's wages of approximately $88.00 for that Saturday. The whole meeting took less than five minutes.

I knew that my decision was the first grievance decision that didn't support my management team and I knew the operations manager was irritated. I asked her to stay behind as the others left the conference room. I let her vent about paying someone for not working. As sure as she was that her position was correct, I was as certain that my decision was the only one I could make. I explained that no one should be penalized for the ineptitude of our business. No one should be penalized because we didn't know how to get a simple piece of paper from one end of our building to the other end.

I also mentioned that I had an excellent working relationship with the union's business agent. I firmly believed that, if he didn't win a few grievances, we would have a new business agent who wasn't easy to work with. In dealing with the union we would be honest and fair and they would win a few. I know I didn't sway her that day, but it was the start of a new culture that I knew was long overdue in that business.

* * * *

I was in charge of closing a business whose workers were represented by a union. We manufactured 380 distinct parts which we were transferring to our other plants. We decided to send two parts, less than 1%, to our plant in Mexico.

The Mexican plant insisted that it send a few people to the plant we were closing to observe the manufacture of the two parts and to train on the equipment. Everyone back at headquarters anticipated major problems if the workers from Mexico came into the plant. They came and there were no problems.

Prior to scheduling their visit, we met with the union stewards. We explained that since we were sending two parts to Mexico, again less than 1%, all workers in the plant could apply for additional unemployment benefits and re-training benefits under NAFTA. We also explained that we would try to train with volunteers from our plant. Everyone agreed to proceed.

On the Monday when the workers from Mexico arrived, we had coffee and donuts in the conference room for the visitors as well as the people who had volunteered to train them. Management and the union stewards gathered also. Everyone gathered to meet each other and spend a few minutes getting to know each other a little better. Then we all went to work.

On Friday morning, one of the stewards asked to meet with me. The people who were training the Mexican workers wanted to know if it was okay to take the visitors sightseeing on Saturday and cook some hamburgers in someone's backyard for everyone on Sunday.

I was amazed. People who were obviously concerned about their jobs disappearing in a few months were concerned about the people who were taking two of those jobs away. And the union officials were carrying the message to me.

During the plant closing, we were treating our people with compassion and fairness. We all had difficult things to do and were working together to do them.

As we reached the final days of operation, I started receiving e-mails and notes from the employees. All thanked me for being honest with them, being fair to them, and for treating them with dignity.

No matter how tough the job and no matter how tough the union, your chances of success are enhanced when you try to work with the unions. Being honest and fair, but also firm, will help you in that quest.

It doesn't always work. Some unions think they need to be militant. There is not much you can do to change this. I have found though that it is always worthwhile to at least try to work with them.

Lesson 31

BE A FAMILY

I'll always remember my first visit to one of our plants whose results were far superior to our second-best plant. Since it was my first visit to that business, a plant tour was part of my agenda.

The tour took a little longer than most plant tours. The reason was that the president of the business stopped at each machine to talk to the operator. At one he knew that the operator's father had recently been hospitalized and he asked how Dad was doing. At another, he knew that the operator's son had a big ball game the night before and he wanted to know the results of the game. At another an operator was getting married in a week and he asked how the wedding plans were going. At another machine, nothing big was happening in the operator's life but he engaged in some small talk anyway. He stopped a fork lift and asked the driver about a recent vacation.

The president knew everyone on the floor and in the office. He knew something that was going on in the lives of everyone in the business. And he seemed to truly care about everyone in his plant.

He established a simple culture in his workplace. That culture was that all the employees were part of one large extended family. Families care about everyone in the family. By his example, he established the work force as a family. As the day progressed, I witnessed the family camaraderie in the break room, in the offices, and everywhere else I went.

Months later, I was asked why I thought that business did so much better than the others. I answered that it had the ingredients of a good business. It had a capable leader and a skilled staff. The leader had a vision and inspired the troops to fulfill that vision. The one factor that set it apart from the other businesses however was a sense of being one big family that cared about the other members of the family.

With all the privacy concerns and laws of today's society, it may seem tricky to gain all the personal knowledge of others that the president of that business possessed. The laws prevent you from prying into the personal lives of your employees, but they don't prevent you from talking to others. You can not ask an employee (or prospective employee) if he or she is married. However, if in the course of a conversation, a person voluntarily tells you that he or she is married, then you haven't violated any privacy law.

I admired the culture established in that business. I felt it contributed to the success of the business. I have tried to establish that same culture whenever I have found myself leading a business.

The first step is meeting every last person in the business and remembering everyone by their name. The second step is to engage everyone in a little conversation when you see them. Start with talk of the business or that person's job. Let the conversation turn a little to the personal side by volunteering something about yourself or discussing something going on in the community. Talk for a few seconds about the high school football team and you might just discover that the quarterback is the son of the person with whom you are talking. When you learn things about your people, make an effort to remember them.

Whenever someone in the organization has a birthday, send a card a few days before the birthday. Start a newsletter and include births, birthdays, and other events in the lives of your business family.

Whatever you do in establishing a family culture, make certain that you are including everyone. If you have three shifts, make sure you visit the off-shifts so everyone is included. You would be better doing nothing than trying to establish a family culture and excluding a number of people. You must treat everyone alike or you are flirting with disaster.

You and everyone else spend at least forty hours together each week. You are a family in a sense by virtue of the time you spend together. Treat people like they are part of the family. You will see the results.

Lesson 32

COMMITMENTS

Did you ever hear about the chicken and the hog that were walking down the road together? They spotted a new billboard for a local restaurant that had a huge picture of a plate of ham, eggs, and hash browns. The chicken turned to the hog and said, "Doesn't that make you proud?"

The hog replied, "Not really. That plate only requires a contribution from you. It requires a total commitment from me!"

That, to me, is one of the best definitions of the word commitment. When you tell anyone you are going to do something, you are making a commitment. You need to do everything you can, short of giving your life, to meet that commitment.

People to whom you make a commitment depend upon you to meet that commitment. They trust you to meet that commitment. They respect you when you meet that commitment. And when you don't keep that commitment, they lose respect for you and they lose trust in you. When that happens, it is tremendously hard to ever win back their trust and respect again.

I've met countless people who say they are going to do something and don't follow through. I don't think they know that they are committing themselves to do what they say they will. They don't understand the consequences they face when they break commitments or perhaps, they just don't care.

How many times have you heard someone say, "He talks the talk, but I don't see him walking the walk"? I've heard it so many times that it confirms my suspicion that a lot of people tell you they are going to do something but they don't follow through. I know of two people who were terminated because they continually promised to do things and never followed through.

A new plant manager came to a plant in which I spent a lot of time. During his first week he got off to a great start. He had several meetings with different groups of employees to introduce himself to them, to discuss his vision of where he wanted to take the plant, and to answer any questions they might have. Unfortunately, he told them he would get onto the floor on all three shifts, get to know the people, and within a few months he would know everyone by their name.

After the first week he got very busy on something because he never got out of his office. The employees started to grumble that he wasn't keeping the commitments he made to them during his first week. The foremen took the complaints directly to the plant manager and told him he really needed to make an effort to get out of his office and get to know the people. In spite of this direct feedback, he never seemed to have the time to do what he had said he would do.

The plant had birthday lunches each month. All employees who had a birthday that month came to the conference room for lunch, birthday cake, and a few words from the plant manager. At one birthday lunch, almost a year after the plant manager's arrival, he rose to give his little birthday speech. Before he could say a word, one of the employees jumped up and asked, "Who are you?"

The plant manager told them that he was the plant manager. The employee said, "Oh yeah, now I recognize you. You never came out to get to know us and I had forgotten what you looked like".

In spite of that little jab, he still never got out to the floor very much and the employees continued to be upset that he hadn't kept his word. They never forgave him and never forgot. When contract negotiations rolled around, the union committee refused to meet with the plant manager because they claimed that they couldn't trust anything he said. They were overreacting; however, he had made a commitment that he didn't keep. When you do that, people will lose their respect for you.

Good sales people can tell you the value of keeping your commitments. I've been told by more than one sales person that, "When I go out into the field, I have only my name and my good word. If I lose my good word, I go into the field with nothing".

Be careful when you tell someone that you will do something. Make sure that you can do it. Remember that you are making a commitment. And remember that you must do everything you can, short of killing yourself, to meet your commitments. "It ain't okay to fail" in your commitments.

Lesson 33

KEEP IT SIMPLE, STUPID

"Keep it simple, stupid" is a philosophy that is fairly prevalent in business. It is popular enough that it has become known by its acronym "KISS". I have heard it many times in many businesses. The problem is that, in spite of so many people advocating "KISS", I don't see many people following it.

The best example of not following it could be the automotive industry. I own an older car which has a book value of approximately $12,000. I recently noticed that a small amount of oil was leaking onto my driveway and I took the car to the shop to see what was leaking. They told me that the oil was leaking around a seal that needed to be replaced. They estimated it would be a two day job and would cost $1,800! I couldn't believe that it would cost 15% of the value of the car to replace a one-dollar oil seal. The reason the job would be so expensive was that the transmission had to be removed in order to have access to the oil seal. The yo-yo that designed that vehicle apparently had no desire to keep the design simple.

In the 1980's I was leading a business which supplied automotive light bulbs to each of the American automobile companies. Engineers from one of the companies met with us to see what could be done to make 100% of the dashboard lights last one full year. We guaranteed 99.9%

would last a year, but that wasn't good enough. We learned that the need to have every last dashboard light work through the one-year warranty period was because of the difficulty and costs associated with changing the bulb. Incredibly, this particular vehicle had been designed in such a manner that both front doors and the windshield had to be removed in order to get behind the dashboard. It took four hours to change a light bulb in the dashboard. Once again, no one followed the philosophy of "Keep it Simple, Stupid."

When I was a young engineer designing aircraft engines, "KISS" was a design standard. The leader of that business had been an aircraft mechanic for the Flying Tigers during World War II. His hands were severely scarred from burns he received while replacing worn parts in hard-to-reach places on hot engines. He insisted that all our designs be such that maintenance could be simple. As many parts that would wear as possible had to be easily accessible. If there was more than one way to design a component, the simplest way was required. If you wanted to lose your job, all you had to do was design something that was too complicated, hard to reach, or hard to maintain.

As I look at the estimate to replace the one dollar seal on my automobile I wish that the philosophy of "KISS" which I worked under could have been introduced into the automotive industry.

The good and bad examples of "KISS" have been in the context of design. However, every aspect of your work and your business can benefit from the "KISS" philosophy. Anything you do that can be done in more than one way can benefit.

Suppose you have a business trip from New York to Los Angeles. You could fly from New York to Chicago, catch a train from there to Albuquerque and take a bus from there to Los Angeles. Or you could take a direct flight from New York to Los Angeles. The no-brainer, simple alternative is the direct flight.

In your work, you might develop a spreadsheet to do some analysis, you might put together a presentation, you might write a business letter, or you might plan a project. There are a number of ways you can accomplish each. The simplest way to do each is always the best way.

In your business you have a number of systems, such as accounting systems and payroll systems. Paperwork for shipping, receiving, and purchasing can be cumbersome. You need to look at all systems and aspects of your business to see what can be simplified. What can be made simpler? If something can be done more simply, do it because it will make everyone's work easier.

I recommend an exercise in flow charting. Take something like an order coming in to your business. Map the process of what happens from the time you get an order to the time when you ship product, invoice it and get payment. Determine the steps in the process and draw each step on a large sheet of paper. Draw connecting lines showing how work flows from one person to another and from one department to another. Show everyone who touches and impacts the process of filling that order and getting paid for it. Show every piece of paper that is generated. You will be surprised at how complicated the map becomes.

My guess is that there will be lots of people, processes, and paper. It would not be surprising if one piece of paper crossed the same person's desk two or three times on its journey. The lines on your map may crisscross and start to look like a plate of spaghetti. Your business process and flow may be far from simple. If it is, you have taken the first step in applying "KISS". The process map will show you areas where things can be simplified to make jobs easier and to reduce some of the costs of doing business.

This exercise can be applied to other aspects of your business. Map the flow of a new product through conception, design, prototype, and production. Map your time, attendance and payroll system. These maps will help you streamline your business and reduce your costs.

If there is more than one way to do your work, to design your products or to run your business systems, the simple way will always be the best way. It will make jobs easier, your products better, and will help reduce your costs.

As you approach your work and business, always remember and apply "KISS". KEEP IT SIMPLE, STUPID.

Lesson 34

THE FLAT ORGANIZATION

When I joined GE in 1969, it was a huge company with a multitude of management layers. A factory worker reported to a foreman who reported to an assembly manager who reported to a plant manager. The plant manager reported to a manufacturing manager who reported to a department general manager. The general manager reported to a division vice-president who reported to the group executive. The group executive reported to a sector executive who reported to a vice-chairman who reported to the chairman of the board.

The hierarchy of organizational groups was sub-units, units, subsections, sections, departments, divisions, groups, sectors, and the executive offices. There were nine distinct management layers between the factory worker and the Chairman of the Board.

As a young engineer, I and my colleagues would look at organization charts and wonder what each layer of management actually did. We would ask ourselves why we needed nine layers of management to guide us and our little segment of the business. We asked about the value that each layer could possibly bring to the business.

I think there had to be a full-time employee somewhere in our business segment whose job was to maintain the organization chart. It was published as an elaborate poster complete with photographs of each manager. The chart was constantly changing and was issued with regularity.

The whole thing was laughable to us. When we would leave our office, we would tell the secretary, "If one of our many managers should call, make sure you get his name as well as his phone number".

I had joined GE from the federal government where I had been an engineer for the U.S. Navy Department. As an entry level engineer, I had only six layers of management between me and the President of the United States. At GE I had eight layers of management between me and the chairman.

In the government we had fifteen pay grades. At GE there were twenty-eight pay grades. And the government was considered to be the bloated bureaucracy?

Shortly after Jack Welch took the helm of GE, he announced that we were a bloated bureaucracy with too many management layers. He was going to fix that problem by eliminating layers of management and flatten the organization. He started at the top and quickly eliminated the sector level. These high level executives disappeared from the organization chart.

As he proceeded, communications improved and the enterprise became more agile and efficient. Prior to flattening, it was not uncommon for an Appropriation Request (AR) for a major project to require twenty-five approval signatures. Obtaining that many high level approvals took months. It seemed to take as long to get project approvals as it did to perform the project. It was insane.

After flattening the organization, AR's required only five signatures. Bureaucratic approval documents took weeks rather than months.

The benefits of flattening the organization are many. Jack articulates them extremely well in his book Winning. I won't repeat them here; however I will discuss one benefit which he discusses.

When an organization is flattened by de-layering, managers find themselves with more direct reports. Where before, they had about five direct reports, they may now find themselves with ten to fifteen direct reports. This is great because the manager with fifteen reports just doesn't have the time to "meddle" with the people who are doing their jobs well. He must devote his energies and time to working with the people who need his help. While there are numerous benefits to flattening organizations, this is the greatest in my mind.

You need to examine your organization. Are there too many layers? Does each layer add value to the organization? Do your managers have five direct reports instead of fifteen? How many approvals are required for appropriation requests? Do you want your business to be more agile and efficient?

The answers to these questions may be a signal that you need to flatten your organization. If so, try it. You may like it.

Lesson 35

OBEY THE RULES

On the door to the maintenance department at a die cast company in Jonesboro, Arkansas, is a small sign which is written in the format of a standard warning sign you would find posted on machinery. It says,

"IF YOU THINK OSHA IS A SMALL TOWN IN WISCONSIN, YOU ARE IN BIG TROUBLE."

This is so true!

Businesses must obey the rules published by a multitude of federal and state regulatory agencies. Many executives feel that the regulations are too demanding, too costly, and unnecessary. In short, they feel the regulations are a pain in a particular area of their anatomy.

I believe that the regulations are necessary because some of our predecessors were abusive. They abused the safety and health of their employees. They abused the environment. They abused the safety of the products they made.

When you abuse something, you invite the government to implement regulations to protect the people you are abusing. It is well-known that the pendulum swings through the middle, on its journey from one extreme to the other, at its most rapid speed. It should also be well-known that when the government has to step in with regulations, things go from one extreme to the other. The result can be over-regulation. Don't blame the regulators, but blame the abusers who invited the government regulations in the first place.

If you are an executive who believes the regulations are a pain, you need to adjust your attitude. If you feel you can neglect some regulations and not get caught; you need to adjust that thinking also. The regulatory agencies can fine you or close your business, and will win every fight you get into with them. Instead of fighting them, invest that energy into following the rules.

The Occupational Safety and Health Administration (OSHA) was established to assure the safety and health of America's workers by setting and enforcing standards, providing training, and forming partnerships with American business. OSHA was undoubtedly formed because the safety and health of workers at the time were not high enough priorities for some businesses.

Whenever I led a business, I demanded that our workplace be safe. I always appointed a safety committee of employees to frequently tour the shop and identify anything that would compromise the workers' safety. I supported the committee's recommendations, even though many carried a financial price tag. I did all of this, not to avoid OSHA's fines, but because I cared about the safety of our employees. I didn't want one employee to be hurt on my watch.

The Environmental Protection Agency (EPA) was established to protect human health and the environment. The EPA was undoubtedly formed because protecting the environment at the time was not a high enough priority for some businesses.

We have but one planet on which to live. That should be reason enough to protect the environment.

If your business is in the food products industry, you have two more regulatory agencies helping you. Both the U.S. Department of Agriculture (USDA) and the Food and Drug Administration (FDA) have rules to assure that the public has safe food. These rules were undoubtedly formulated because food safety at times in the past was not a high enough priority for some businesses.

Follow the USDA and FDA rules, not to avoid fines and shutdowns, but because you care about the health of your customers.

The Securities and Exchange Commission (SEC) was formed to protect investors and maintain the integrity of the securities markets. Follow their rules, not to avoid a heavy fine or incarceration, but because you care about your stockholders.

If necessary, you need to adjust your thinking. Follow the rules not to avoid fines, business closure, or incarceration. Follow the rules because you care about your employees, your customers, your shareholders, and your world. All are too valuable to fail.

* * * *

There is another set of rules which are also backed by federal legislation. These are the rules preventing discrimination and harassment in the workplace. They differ from the previous rules in that they don't protect safety and health but rather protect the human dignity of your employees and applicants. They also differ in that you, as the business leader, have a heavy hand in enforcing them yourself. That is precisely what you should do because no one deserves to have his or her dignity attacked when they come to work

One day, the president of a company for which I worked stopped by my office and asked me to go with him in case he needed some help. On the way to the factory floor he explained to me that he had just received a call that two people were having an altercation in the factory. When we arrived, the two men were close to throwing punches. One was a white person and the other was a black person. When the president stepped in and started asking questions, he learned that the altercation started when the white person referred to the black person by the "N" word. When the white person admitted that he said that, the president fired him on the spot.

The reason that the president could act so swiftly is that all employees had previously been informed (verbally and in writing) of the company's zero tolerance position regarding violations of discrimination and harassment policies and that the violator admitted saying the racial slur. It was well-known that the first offense could result in termination. New employees were given the same speech and letter during their first day at work during an orientation session so no one could claim to be unaware of the policies.

The president cared about the dignity of his employees and made it very clear to all that attacks upon anyone's dignity would be dealt with harshly. I admired him for his strong stance. I admired him even more when he backed his words with his actions.

No one in your organization should have their dignity attacked. You, as a leader, should announce that you are drawing a zero tolerance line in the sand. Anyone who practices discrimination or sexual harassment crosses that line and will be dealt with harshly. If anyone is stupid enough to cross that line, you must back up your words by your actions.

If you draw that line in the sand it is important that every one of your employees is informed of the policies. You need to do this in meetings, followed up by individual letters to the people. Document that each person has been informed.

If there are alleged violations, and no one admits guilt, your human resource manager needs to investigate the charges in a professional manner and may need to seek legal counsel. If the charges are substantiated, you need to take action, again in a professional manner.

It is your responsibility to assure that the human dignity of your employees is not attacked. It is just as important as ensuring their safety and health in your workplace.

Lesson 36

INVOLVE YOUR CUSTOMER

In the 1980's the Ford Motor Company decided to explore the possibility of redesigning the S8 tail lamp and turn signal. The engineers at Ford wanted to change the brass bayonet base to a plastic rectangular base. This change would prevent the base from rusting and would allow easier assembly into the automobile. Ford contacted GE, the supplier of the tail lamp, with the request.

GE accepted the request from Ford and started to put together a project plan. The plan included redesigning the light bulb and its base, testing the newly designed lamp for performance and life, designing and building modifications to the manufacturing equipment, and developing a manufacturing process to produce the light bulb.

GE decided to do something novel in this project. Since GE Lighting headquarters and Ford headquarters were only a few hours apart by car travel, GE invited Ford engineers to participate as members of the GE project team. Ford agreed to supply two engineers to GE's project.

Ford and GE engineers worked together on all phases of the project. The results were outstanding because:

1. Ford engineers provide a new, fresh perspective to product design which complemented GE's expertise in light bulbs and resulted in a superior design.
2. Ford engineers were well versed in the newly designed electrical fixture in the automobile. This allowed the design to move more rapidly since exchange of critical design data occurred more quickly than if the teams worked separately.
3. Ford engineers provided valuable input into the design of the equipment modifications.
4. Ford was always aware of progress throughout the program and was never surprised by any variances.
5. When problems occurred, Ford participated in problem solving sessions and provided additional brain power, allowing for better solutions.

When the light bulb started its production ramp-up, Ford engineers stood beside GE engineers and helped with the ramp-up.

It was an outstanding project with outstanding results. All of us felt that a major factor in our success was having Ford so involved in all aspects of the project.

If you are starting a new project with a customer, open your doors and ask the customer to participate as a full team member. Have the customer's engineers sit side by side with your engineers as they design a new product. You will be pleasantly surprised at the outcome of the project as well as with the improved communication throughout the project.

If you choose not to involve the customer as intimately as GE did with Ford on the new tail lamp, at least involve customer in your weekly progress reviews. Patch the customer in on a conference call while you are conducting the review. It will eliminate surprises and will enhance the exchange of information. It also demonstrates that the customer is important and is part of your team. As I have managed several large projects, I have included every customer in weekly progress meetings.

Look for other ways in which you can involve your customer. Your customer doesn't want you to fail and will do all he can to make sure you don't.

Lesson 37

SURROUND YOURSELF WITH THE BEST PEOPLE

I was watching MSNBC's Headliners and Legends show and the subject was Wayne Newton. I was unaware that Wayne Newton, early in his career, was an act in Jack Benny's night club show. A friend of Jack Benny urged him to be careful of Wayne Newton. The friend felt that Wayne had so much talent that, if Jack Benny was not careful, Wayne Newton would replace him as the headline act. Jack Benny told his friend that he wasn't worried. He didn't want anybody in his show if that person didn't have the talent to replace him. Jack Benny wanted no one but the best to participate in his show.

Business leaders should have the same philosophy. They should surround themselves with nothing but the best people. They should also be confident enough in their own abilities that they do not worry about being replaced.

I've known many business leaders who have been highly successful. One of the reasons for their success was that their staffs were made up of the best, most talented people they could find.

Everyone who climbs the business ladder almost immediately reaches a point where they can not do the work by themselves. They must delegate work to the members of their staffs. They will be successful only if the team does its job successfully. Why then wouldn't a business leader want only the best on their team?

I worked for a manager who had four people on his staff. He had an engineering manager, a quality assurance manager, a human resource manager, and me, a program management manager. Whenever he introduced us to others he would add that, "each of these managers is the best in the world at what they do". Each of us was very good at what we did but weren't sure we were "the best in the world".

The manager repeated that accolade on numerous occasions. I came to think he truly meant what he said. True or not, what he was telling people at a minimum was that his staff was comprised of truly outstanding people and that if you placed your work with us you would have nothing but the best working for you.

What he was telling me was that he was a strong, confident manager. He was going to surround himself with the best people. He was going to do that because he wanted the best possible, most successful results from his organization. My odds of accomplishing that objective will be enhanced if I have the best possible people in my organization.

I include this as a lesson because I have seen some mangers that don't try to get the best people they can get. I've even seen a manager who interviewed a young super-star and concluded that he couldn't use the super-star in his organization. It was obvious to many that the super-star could make a great contribution to the organization. We concluded that there was another reason why the manager didn't want the super-star. We suspected that the manager didn't think he needed someone who might shine brighter than himself. That manager was doomed to a career of mediocrity and probably had advanced as far as he would get.

Good managers hire the best possible people they can get. The great managers work to "grow" those people. They provide opportunities to expand their experiences. They coach their subordinates so that their performance improves. They provide training so that their people become better at what they do. Finally, they support and endorse their subordinates as promotional opportunities become available.

You want your organization to be successful. So hire the best people you can find. Once you get those people, become committed to letting them grow.

Lesson 38

UNDERSTAND YOUR BOOKS

Much of my career has been with large companies or divisions of large companies that are comprised of a number of separate businesses (profit and loss centers). Each of the businesses had a finance manager or controller as part of the staff. I have been amazed that some of the leaders of these businesses did not seem to understand the details of the financial side of the business. They rely on the controller to analyze the financials and make recommendations.

Of course, these leaders understand a simple income statement. They can look at an income statement and are able to understand the broad elements such as sales, cost of goods sold, administrative costs, and income. But some don't seem to understand the difference between expense and capital and how each impacts the business differently. They don't seem to even look at the balance sheet. Again, they rely totally upon the controller to understand the financials for them.

I think the reason for this is that the business leader had a great track record in sales, operations, or other functions. Rarely does a great accountant become the leader of a business. Unfortunately, the great sales person or operations manager may not have much knowledge or experience with the intricacies of the financial side of the business.

155

I have had the opportunity to lead a few businesses on an interim basis until a permanent leader is chosen. The average length of these assignments has been about three months. Usually these businesses had been performing poorly and my task was to keep them above water until the permanent replacement was found. My personal objectives have been to turn them around before the permanent replacement comes on board. I have never considered myself to be a caretaker in these assignments.

Once I get an assignment and before I arrive at the business, I request the financials for the last six months from the business I will be leading. I also request the financials from one or two of our similar, but better performing, businesses. With that data I can compare my new business with the better performing businesses and look for particular measurements which are significantly different on a percentage basis. For instance, if the better performing businesses are spending 20% of gross sales on labor and my new business is spending 35% of sales on labor, I know that I will need to concentrate on labor costs. If you understand the books, you will know a lot about the business before you go through the doors.

This is not to imply that a few hours going through the financials will make you aware of everything happening in a business. The financials will help prioritize your focus and point towards directions you need to explore more fully.

My preliminary analysis of the financials for one business I was about to lead told me that labor was an issue. Sales were substantially below the break-even level and the ratio of indirect to direct labor was twice as high as the other businesses that I had reviewed. I knew that I had to gather a lot more information, but I also knew a layoff would be necessary if the business was to get healthy. Increasing sales would help; however, the indirect to direct ratio told me that the labor force was bloated regardless of the sales.

My suspicions were confirmed shortly after my arrival and I developed a one-month plan to accomplish a layoff. The plan involved having meetings with all of the employees to inform them of the financial status of the business, the areas where we needed to find ways to improve, and the fact that layoffs would unfortunately be necessary. The plan also called for a series of meetings with key members of the staff. We would, as a team, decide how many people we needed to run the business. We would then decide, in a very fair and objective manner, the names of those who would be affected by the layoff.

Everything went smoothly with only one exception. When the management team met to determine the names, everyone wanted to lay off the purchasing manager, who wasn't a participant in our layoff meetings. The discussions were emotional and centered on the perception that she was not doing her job. Apparently she would order quantities less than were requested. In many cases she wouldn't even place orders for items requested.

I was shocked that the discussion was so emotional and that the perception was so unanimous. I explained that we couldn't lay her off because she would have call-back rights for six months according to our rules. If we were to lay her off, we could not fill the position with a replacement for six months. If there was a performance problem, I would have to solve it by some other means than a layoff. I promised to follow up on it on a priority basis.

The next day I sat with the purchasing manager and asked if she ordered quantities less than requested and, in some cases, didn't order requested items at all. She admitted that both were correct. When I asked her why she did this, her answer literally floored me.

I learned that my predecessor told her that she could only spend 5% of the estimated revenue each month. He told her that if she exceeded that amount she would be fired. She cut quantities in order to reduce monthly costs, and as each month neared its end and she approached her limit, she had no choice but to stop purchasing items.

I was floored for two reasons. First, the job of a purchasing manager is always to purchase everything that is on a purchase requisition that has been signed (approved) by the business leader. The purchasing manager's value to the business is to get the best possible deal on purchased items. The second reason I was floored was because my predecessor apparently did not understand what impacted the income statement in our business.

His primary measurement was EBIT (earnings before interest and taxes). We were a manufacturing business. Most of our purchases each month were for spare parts and replacement parts for our manufacturing equipment and went through our tool crib. As is typical in a manufacturing business, these parts, if not consumed immediately, go into the tool crib's inventory under accepted accounting procedures. The actual purchase of items impacted cash flow and working capital, but did not impact EBIT until they were used.

My predecessor thought he was impacting the income statement by cutting purchases when, in fact, he was hurting the income. He was not allowing the purchasing manager to get the best possible deal by ordering economically sized lots. He was also driving up the cost of parts because many eventually had to be ordered on a rush basis using premium next-day freight services. He was costing the company more money because he apparently didn't understand the accounting procedures and the financial statements of this business.

Truth is stranger than fiction and this example, though hard to believe, is the absolute truth. My guess is that my predecessor is not unique. I'm sure there are other managers who rely on the controller to sort out and analyze the details of the financial statements. In the meantime, the leader is issuing edicts to staff members which impact the business negatively because he doesn't understand the books.

I recommend that anyone who aspires to be a manager or a business leader take an introductory course in accounting. Such a course is usually available at a local college or from a local adult education program. If nothing is available from those sources, search for a correspondence course or something on-line. Find something that will give you an overview of business financials.

I also recommend that, regardless of your position, you sit with your finance manager and ask him to show you the key financial reports and walk you through the items. When reviewing the statements, make a list of items you'd like to learn more about. You will be looking at summary reports and might ask about the details. A line item in an income statement may represent the total of a number of journal entries. Who makes the journal entries? How are they entered into the financial programs? Who does the data entry? Is that person accurate? What checks and balances are utilized to ensure accuracy of the report? How is the report reconciled? What sanity checks can you apply to the report to have confidence it makes sense?

There is one additional compelling reason for you to understand your financial results and assure that they are accurate. Your financial statements feed into the overall corporate results. The Sarbanes-Oxley legislation requires that your corporate leader sign and attest to the accuracy of the corporate financial statement. The penalties for inaccurate statements are severe. For that reason, your contribution to the corporate financial statement needs to be completely accurate.

As a business leader, the financial reports are your score card. You need to spend the time to make sure they are accurate. You need to spend the time to understand your score card thoroughly. Most importantly, you really need to know how your decisions impact the bottom line. If you don't, you will fail. But you know by now that "it ain't okay to fail".

Lesson 39

CONFLICT

If you are a business leader, you probably have a staff of people reporting to you who lead the various departments in your organization. In a traditional business those departments are sales and marketing, engineering, manufacturing, finance or accounting, human resources, and administration.

These departments have several tasks that they work on independently. That work can be performed solely by the people in a particular department without assistance from the other departments to perform those tasks. For instance, the sales and marketing department can change the boundaries of the different sales territories without help from any other department. Likewise, engineering can write a maintenance manual for one of your products by itself and manufacturing can receive orders and develop a production schedule by itself.

There are also a number of tasks performed by the business that require various departments to work together. In preparing operating budgets, the finance department needs input from all departments. When the preliminary budget is determined and exceeds what the business can spend, finance works with all departments to change their input.

When engineering designs a new product, it must work closely with both the sales and manufacturing departments. The sales department understands the market and must impact the design to make sure the new product can be sold. Manufacturing must insist on a design that can be economically produced.

If one department needs to discipline or terminate an employee, it must work with the human resource department to assure that laws are obeyed and that the person's rights are not violated.

In most tasks that require more than one department, there is inherent conflict. On the new product, sales wants one design, manufacturing wants something else, and neither coincides with the design that engineering has developed. The solution is that the different parties must try to compromise.

Most tasks which involve more than one department have the potential of conflict. When conflict develops at the lower levels of your organization, it will usually rise to the department managers' level fairly rapidly. The reason for this is that the junior levels can't compromise. If they do compromise, they are giving something away in the process and not obtaining their desired result. They won't do this because they think the department head will be upset with them when they give something away.

As the business leader you have no problem with conflicts rising to the department head level. After all, you pay each of your department heads very well. They are strong, competent people and you know that they can work together and reach compromises. You expect them to do just that and not bother you with these conflicts. You are too busy to get involved in resolving conflicts in the organization.

Your thinking is about 95% correct. As a rule of thumb, 95% of the conflicts arising in your business can be satisfactorily resolved by your people. Conversely, about 5% of the conflicts can not be resolved by your department heads. Those conflicts must ultimately come to your attention for resolution.

A hypothetical case in which you had to become involved would be parking meters. You produce and sell a standard parking meter which is painted with a silver powder coat. These parking meters have a maximum time of two hours. The marketing organization has been talking to numerous cities about creating some longer term parking, allowing a maximum of eight hours, several blocks from the town center. This would create more parking revenue for the cities and would have a quick payback of the cost of the new meters. The only catch is that they would want the long term meters to be painted red so the motorist could quickly identify the long term parking spots.

Marketing has discussed this incremental sales opportunity with engineering and sales, and everyone is excited about the potential new revenue. When they discuss the opportunity with manufacturing, they hit a brick wall. Manufacturing has a paint line which currently uses only silver paint. If the business was to introduce an additional color, manufacturing would be faced with lengthy change-overs from one color to the other, which would negatively impact their efficiency measurements. This conflict between marketing and manufacturing has no compromise and the two managers can not resolve the conflict. The red parking meter conflict has to come to your attention for resolution.

This is not bad. It should not reflect poorly on the managers because they could not resolve the issue themselves and had to get you involved. It is merely part of the 5% of conflicts that will require your involvement.

As a business leader you must accept the fact that 5% of the conflicts within your organization will come to your attention for a decision. Look for and anticipate a certain level of conflict to hit your office.

If no conflict ever reaches your office, you need to be concerned. When absolutely no conflicts reach your office, you can be certain that you have one manager who is bullying the other managers or you have some weak willed managers who are caving to avoid conflicts. If no conflicts reach your office you have a problem in your managerial ranks and you need to deploy your antenna.

Lesson 40

THE SKUNK AWARD

I know a woman who once worked as a sales associate for a nationally-known department store. Each sales associate was assigned to a particular department and was responsible for keeping the department neat and tidy.

There were times during heavy selling seasons and clearance sales when the departments got messy. There were also some departments in which the associates could care less about housekeeping.

The store's management came up with a little program that they thought would address the housekeeping issues. They bought a small figurine of a skunk and awarded the skunk each week to the department that was the messiest. I guess this was management's way of telling you that your department "stunk". If you won this award you had to display the skunk on your cash register until the following week. Additionally, if you got the award, you were sent home early that day without pay. I kid you not. That was the program.

If you get to know the sales associates in a large department store, you will find some live from paycheck to paycheck and can not afford an afternoon off without pay. The program worked very well with this population and their departments were kept very clean and tidy.

There is another group of sales associates who do not work because of the money. Their children are grown and have left home. These people are there to have something to do other than sit at home all day watching television. The money is nice but it is not the motivation for working. This group didn't care if they got the skunk award and had to display it on their cash registers. Some actually asked, "What exactly do I need to do to get the skunk award and have an afternoon off?"

I have found that negative programs have mixed results and never achieve the objectives you hope for. I'll go as far to say that most positive incentive programs also have mixed results, particularly if they reward individuals.

Giving a favored parking space to the "employee of the month" generally makes one person pretty happy. It also makes a bunch of other employees disappointed, or even mad, because they didn't get named as "employee of the month". Each felt they were more deserving than the winner. The reason this type of program doesn't work is that selection is usually based on subjective rather than objective criteria.

Giving a baseball cap to the person who submitted the best suggestion each month has the same effect. What constitutes the best suggestion? What quantifiable measurements are applied to determine which suggestion is best? If you put in suggestions each month and none are deemed to be the best, how long will you continue submitting suggestions?

The incentive programs that work the best are those that reward the whole team when a business objective is met. Those programs don't single out individuals and thus help to build a team atmosphere.

The best program I've observed was one in a business for which I worked many years ago. A matrix was established with percent of targeted revenue heading each column and percent of targeted net income in each row. The percentages went from 100% to 110%. In each cell was a percentage that varied from 1% to 10% and represented a bonus commensurate with the results. At the end of each quarter the revenue and net income were announced as percentages of the targets. If both targets were met or exceeded, every employee got a small bonus in the amount determined by the spreadsheet. Everyone knew what the targets were and everyone worked hard each quarter to exceed the targets. Everyone wanted to get the maximum 10% bonus. People paid attention to the operation and searched for ideas to make it better. Everyone worked hard and we had one of the best working environments I've ever seen.

I saw another program in one of our businesses in which all employees participated. If monthly income was met, the program paid a bonus to each employee. The amount was based on a formula that included four factors: manufacturing efficiencies, scrap, downtime and safety. This program also worked well.

The key to the success of these programs is to publish the numbers weekly. Let the people know where the business stands in terms of sales, income, safety, and whatever other factors determine the bonuses. Let everyone know where the bonus is landing and what must be done to improve it before the end of the month or quarter.

These all inclusive incentive programs cost more than a baseball cap or a figurine of a skunk. But they have a positive effect on the employees' morale and performance, which is what you are seeking. They build teamwork. They also yield some pretty good incremental benefits to the business results.

Lesson 41

THE BEATINGS WILL CONTINUE

I once saw a sign that said, "The beatings will continue until the morale improves".

It reminds me so much of several managers I've had over the years that think autocracy is the best way to manage. The autocratic manager is the one who apparently feels he must micro-manage his troops in order to get the maximum results. He yells at, harasses, and threatens his employees almost all of the time. If he doesn't have a few employees on the brink of a nervous breakdown, he doesn't feel he is doing his job very well. I believe another word for this type of manager is "jerk".

The people in an autocratic environment are not allowed to think. They are told what to do, when to do it, and are allowed to do no more or no less.

It is surprising to me that the autocrat never realizes how much more he could get from his employees if only he treated them like human beings. It is even more surprising to me that there are so many of these characters still operating today. In my travels, I have run across a few in just the past year.

The reason why it is so surprising that this type of manager is still around is that good companies recognized years ago that the way to maximize an organization's performance is to empower the people and let them loose. The good manager is the one that sets the goals, articulates the vision, gets out of the way, and spends his time coaching the team instead of yelling at it.

It has been over fifteen years since I led a series of classes for GE managers called "Processes". One of the classes involved dividing into two teams and spending some time building paper airplanes.

Each team started with paper cutters, paper folders, quality inspectors, and flight testers. Every plane that flew a certain number of feet in a fairly straight line was deemed acceptable and counted in inventory. Planes that failed the flight test were scrapped and not counted in inventory.

Everything was identical for each team with one exception. One team had a manager who had been given instructions to be autocratic. People could only do what he told them. They could not talk to each other. He was to constantly yell at them to make more planes.

The other manager was enabling. His people could talk to each other. Everyone on that team was encouraged to come up with ideas that would improve production. The manager was instructed to be lenient in letting people try different ways to improve.

You know the rest of the story. The team with the autocrat always lost the game. There was no need to rig the results. The team with the enabling manager always had five times more airplanes at the end of the day than the other team.

During and after the game we would stop and ask for discussions regarding how people felt on each team. I don't remember specific comments. I do remember some of the discussions were not pretty.

That was fifteen years ago. Today I would guess not one company in America is so in the dark that it doesn't know autocracy is not the way to go. Yet in my travels I see the autocratic manager still in existence, still getting pay raises and bonuses, and still being a jerk.

I think all companies today are talking the talk. Unfortunately, some still need to walk the walk.

Lesson 42

IMMEDIATE IMPROVEMENT

A formal program called "Continuous Improvement" has been developed during the past ten years. It was founded in the correct belief that in order for a business to remain competitive, it had to find ways to continuously improve. In other words, improvement cannot end if you are to remain competitive.

Strong businesses have been continuously improving for many decades without the need to have a formal program. In GE's Lighting Business, we were challenged each year to achieve at least six percent cost productivity improvement over the prior year. We had to identify projects and implement them every year to meet this challenge.

Today, most companies have a Continuous Improvement program to achieve similar results. In fact, in order to meet the International Standards for Quality, companies must have a Continuous Improvement Program.

Some companies appoint a continuous improvement director to coordinate the activities. They appoint a team of managers and employees to identify and evaluate potential projects. Teams are appointed to implement chosen projects. Periodic meetings are held to identify additional projects and to monitor projects that are underway.

Many corporations now have training sessions in continuous improvement techniques. Some appoint a full-time Director of Continuous Improvement to arrange training and to audit the various programs throughout the corporation.

All of this is good for business. It keeps a focus on the operational efficiency of the business and helps to make the business more competitive. If your business does not have a continuous improvement program, I recommend that you consider implementing one. There are many books and courses available on the subject.

As good as continuous improvement can be, I feel another set of procedures can also be developed and implemented by business to augment continuous improvement. I think there also needs to be similar focus on "Immediate Improvement." While projects are the essence of continuous improvement, decisions and directives are the essence of immediate improvement.

Immediate improvement actions are, by definition, those which you think of today, implement tomorrow, and yield benefits the day after tomorrow.

In one plant I worked, operators wore gloves to protect their hands from sharp edges and the heat of the parts they were making. The gloves would wear thin and needed to be replaced every few days. Replacement gloves were stocked in a tool crib near the back of the plant and employees could get a pair whenever they felt they "needed" a replacement.

One of the managers noticed long lines at the tool crib at the start of each shift. He learned that the operators clocked in and went directly to the tool crib for new gloves at the start of each shift. The long lines indicated an inefficiency that needed to be addressed.

After a brief review, the plant manager decided to move replacement gloves to a locked cabinet near the foreman's office. When operators needed gloves, they would tell the foreman who would see that replacement gloves were delivered to the operator within a few minutes.

A couple of things happened. Since operators had to deal with the foreman, they didn't seem to "need" replacement gloves as often. Instead of ordering a few cases of gloves every week, we started ordering a few cases every month. This resulted in a 75% cost reduction in gloves to the business. By eliminating the long lines at the start of each shift, we estimated a 3% gain in productivity. Both of these gains were achieved immediately.

We didn't have to develop a project. We didn't have to invest any capital. We merely made a decision one day, implemented it the next day, and saw the gains the following day. With a simple decision, we had "Immediate Improvement."

In every business, there are many opportunities for immediate improvement as well as continuous improvement. The challenge is to identify the immediate improvement opportunities. Implementing them involves only a simple decision. The question becomes, "How do we identify the immediate improvement opportunities?"

The first step is for you and your staff to carefully observe your business. Are there lines of people anywhere? Are there operations that seem to take a long time? Are people grumbling about something that takes too long to accomplish? Can you see any inefficiencies? Ask a lot of questions until you understand why the operations are as they are.

Ask all of the people in the organization for help. Pull them together in small groups. Ask them to tell you about any procedures that they must follow which could be done smarter or easier. Some will speak out while others will say nothing. However, at the end of the day, you will have a list of opportunities.

After you have a list of concerns, sit down with your staff and brainstorm the opportunities. Which items are necessary and can't be changed? Which items can be changed to make them more efficient? What changes can be implemented to fix the inefficiency? Review the ideas and implement those that make sense. Make the decisions, announce them, and watch for the benefits in a day or so.

This all sounds very simple. The reason for this is that the process for immediate improvement is simple. It is an effort to see the obvious, consider alternatives, and implement the improvement.

Some actions will not get the benefits you envision. Do not worry if this happens because you tried but it didn't work so you're returning to the old procedure. These instances will be rare.

The people in your organization know what things are inefficient and probably know how to fix them. With your encouragement and support they will help you. Many of their ideas will result in benefits to the business.

The focus of "Immediate Improvement" is one of the best tools you can launch in your business. The solutions coming from immediate improvement exercises are implemented quickly and with insignificant costs, if any. The results and benefits are seen immediately.

Implement this focus. Repeat the procedures every six months. Sit back and watch the quick gains in productivity in your business.

<u>Lesson 43</u>

THE IMPERIAL MANAGEMENT TEAM

Why do so many management teams have to be so imperial? Why does the general manager act like a monarch and the staff act like ministers of the Royal Court? Why do they act as if they are entitled to lavish extravagances as a result of their positions? The answer to these questions is that they don't have to operate that way. They choose to act that way.

I'm talking about the seemingly endless perks enjoyed by some upper management teams. I'm talking about the incessant boondoggles and extravagances taken by some executive teams.

Over my career I have been in a few royal courts. I must admit that I was given a few perks and I must also admit that I enjoyed them. In fact, I never refused a perk. I wonder, in retrospect, whether my troops resented my perks. At the time, I never gave it a thought. I should have.

The problem is that whatever you do to keep the perks a secret, the troops become aware of them. While they may motivate the person enjoying them, they can negatively impact the troops. They don't resent

177

the perks; however, they start to resent the managers' attitudes that they are entitled to them because they are better than the troops.

If you are an executive, you are providing more value to your business than the accountants, the sales force, the engineers, the secretaries, the labor force, and everyone else in the organization. All of those people know of your value to the business and also know that you are rewarded with a handsome salary and a nice bonus each year. They don't resent your pay because they know you earned it. But they don't understand your company Corvette or your full membership in the Country Club that you've also been given. They start thinking that the Corvette and Country Club costs could be better used by sharing that money amongst the employees. If so, they could get a few more dollars each month to help pay the electric bill. They start asking why they should work so hard all the time when you're being paid to golf every Friday afternoon.

The practice or policy of management's extravagance must be fairly universal. Jack Welch, again in his book *Winning*, addresses extravagances. He discusses them in the context of becoming a leader. On the day you become a leader, a lot of things change. Maybe you start flying first class instead of coach. Jack reminds everyone that on the day you became a leader, nobody gave you a crown. But I've seen many managers who think they wear a crown.

There is a fine line somewhere that separates the management team that is respected by the troops and the management team that is imperial and not respected as much. I recommend that, in order to get the most from your employees, you try to discover where that line is and you try to stay on the correct side of it.

To help you in that determination, I will employ a modification of Jeff Foxworthy's trademark line.

1. You might just be imperial if you can't entertain customers at the local country club, but must fly them on the company jet to Pebble Beach.

2. You might just be imperial if the local lake is where you take your son to fish, but take customers to fish at one of the rustic, expensive camps within 400 miles of the Arctic Circle with the company footing the bill.
3. You might just be imperial if you send the troops an e-mail to watch their travel expenses and you send it from your suite at the Waldorf Astoria while on a business trip to Madison Square Garden to catch the NIT games.
4. You may just be imperial if your company car is a Corvette. (I once worked for a person whose company car was a brand new Corvette. How practical is a company vehicle with only two seats? Give me a break.)
5. You might just be imperial if your secretary is on crutches recovering from knee surgery and has to hobble from the parking lot two blocks away because there are no parking spaces for the handicapped and you're not about to give her your reserved space next to the front door.
6. You might just be imperial if you take your wife to dinner for two "blue plate specials", but on company business you have nothing less than appetizers, salad, soup, dinner, dessert and a $100 bottle of wine.
7. You might just be imperial if one of your managers has to fly to a city that you are going to visit in a few weeks just to inspect potential hotels for you so that you will be staying at one that has the appropriate pillow firmness and other amenities that you require.
8. You might just be imperial if you visit a plant at which two of the engineers from your office have been working away from home for six months and you don't bother to invite them to have dinner with you.
9. You might just be imperial if the only place that you and your staff can develop a business strategy is a lavish resort.
10. You may just be imperial if the strategy development meeting takes four days because the morning sessions are so draining that the only thing you can do in the afternoon is play golf or fish.

11. You may just be imperial if you finally agree to have a company picnic for the common folk and ask them to make donations to help defray the expense of the event. "We have to keep an eye on that bottom line!"
12. You might just be imperial if the cost to remodel your office exceeds $250,000 and it shows.
13. You might just be imperial if your company car is a limousine and comes with a full-time driver who is also on the company payroll.
14. You might just be imperial if you're attending a big event, traffic is a mess and you send an employee to sit in the traffic jams so he can report back to you about which route is the least congested. This allows you to watch TV in your hotel suite and not waste your valuable time in the traffic. (Hey, your Majesty, you don't have one single employee in your entire business who enjoys sitting in traffic jams, even if they're getting paid to do it.)
15. You might just be imperial if nothing on this list seems wrong or extravagant to you.

The list could easily be longer; however the point has been made. Besides, I wanted the list to reflect only actual items that I know to be true. Nothing on the list is made up or exaggerated. It all happened.

Perks for management are a lot like personal strengths. They become a weakness only when carried to an excess. When that happens, you look like a monarch and not like the business leader you are. Like strengths, you should examine and evaluate your perks and keep them in check. If you don't, your employees will not respect you as much as they could or should and that's nothing but a shame.

Lesson 44

LOYALTY

Sadly, loyalty is a word that no longer seems to be in the lexicon of American business. Decades ago, good employees had an unwavering loyalty to their company. And companies displayed the same unwavering loyalty to their employees. I joined GE in the 1960's with the thought that, if I performed well and was loyal, I would spend the rest of my career at GE. My good friend Andy Bertinelli, a retired General Motors executive, joined his company with the same thoughts. His vision came to be. Mine did not.

In the lesson on networking I discussed in detail the global competitive pressures that changed the dynamics of American business. I also mentioned that loyalty, as we knew it, was a victim of those dynamics.

I won't repeat the details, but I will discuss loyalty from a personal perspective.

First, I need to introduce another friend, Bill Gradison. In a letter to me a few years ago, Bill told me he was starting his seventh distinct career. He had just been appointed by President Bush to the Public Company Accounting Oversight Board, established by the Sarbanes-Oxley Act. Prior to that Bill had been an investment banker, Mayor of Cincinnati, a

U.S, Congressman, and Executive Director of a consortium of insurance companies. We met while he was Mayor of Cincinnati.

Bill is highly educated with an MBA and PhD. from Harvard. He is one of the most honest, ethical people I have ever met. He cares a lot about people and is a genuinely nice person.

I was a vice-mayor in one of Cincinnati's suburbs when Bill made his first run for Congress. It was a special election with the regular election following just five months later. I supported Bill in the first election, but didn't know him personally. I was disappointed when he lost that election by approximately 3,000 votes. He carried Cincinnati but lost the suburbs – my turf.

I felt I knew what he needed to do to turn around the suburban vote in the next election, which was less than five months away. And I felt that if he didn't run his campaign differently, he would end up with the same results. So I called his brokerage firm, introduced myself, asked to speak to him and was surprised when he picked up the phone only seconds later. After a brief conversation, he invited me to lunch the next day.

When we met, I explained that his politics were okay with the suburbanites, but he needed to visit the suburban communities more frequently to demonstrate he cared about their issues. They just didn't get fired up for a candidate because his signs were littering empty fields.

I thought he needed to spend time in each of the twenty-one towns and cities in the suburbs going door-to-door and learning of our issues. I could arrange for the mayor or a councilman in each city to accompany him. I could also arrange for each community's weekly newspaper to photograph him visiting "Mr. Smith's" home and run it on the front page.

By the end of lunch he was excited by the plan and offered me the position of Suburban Campaign Manager which I accepted. I accepted the position, in part because that brief lunch introduced me to a genuinely decent human being, far more so than came across on the television.

We spent countless afternoons from 4 until 7pm going door-to-door. It was tiring but we had so much fun. My 5-year old daughter would go with us many afternoons. At the end of the day, we'd go to a fast food place for a bite to eat. His staff and I would sit at one table planning the next excursion to the suburbs. Debbie and Bill would sit at another table in deep discussions. We were amazed that this future congressman could sit and talk to anyone in the restaurant and campaign, but chose to relax at day's end with a youngster discussing her day.

The election came quickly and Bill won by more than 3,000 votes. I was tickled that we carried the suburbs. We all were delighted. It ain't okay to fail and, by golly, we didn't.

A few years later I was running for re-election. In my community, we all ran as independents, with no party affiliation allowed. I am pretty sure we were all of the same persuasion. I'm certain we all were Gradison supporters. We should have worked well together. That was not the case as we were bitterly divided over the need for a new municipal income tax. There were four of us against the tax and three for it.

We wanted to strengthen our plurality so I took a running mate who was against the tax. He had never run for office before but had a steep learning curve to go through. We took a sample poll midway through the campaign which showed me winning but my running mate losing.

We developed a strategy to goose my running mate's campaign. Part of the strategy was to have Bill Gradison go door-to-door with us on the Friday before the election. That would allow for newspaper coverage hitting the streets on the day before the election.

I called Bill and he agreed to come home from Washington to help us.

I mentioned that all council members supported Bill. For him to campaign for us and not them would irritate them and he knew it. When he campaigned for us it did irritate them and they let him know it. What was more important to Bill was loyalty.

I had been loyal to Bill. I admired him so much and cared about him so much I would have taken a bullet for him. He knew that and he returned the loyalty to me. He was so loyal to me that he didn't hesitate to campaign for me even knowing it could hurt him with some of his other supporters.

Loyalty is a tremendous force. It's great to have it for someone else and it's great to get it from someone else. So why has it seemed to die in business? Has its demise hurt business?

I don't think it is completely dead on the part of business; however, it's hurt pretty badly. The standard of employment-for-life is gone. We understand why that happened. We don't understand companies failing because of corporate greed and scandals. Those leaders, with some doing jail time, have shown loyalty to themselves and no one else in their businesses. Companies eliminating pensions are demonstrating no loyalty to their employees.

As a result, employees are showing little or no loyalty to their employers. Some work 8-to-5 and not a minute more. Some jump from job to job, company to company. After a company invests in them, they leave. This, too, is a lack of loyalty.

This mutual lack of loyalty has to impact business. Employees are not as highly motivated which has to impact results. Constant turnover also has to negatively impact business.

Businesses must search for ways to demonstrate their loyalty to their people. Loyalty is a two-way street. Employees must work on their loyalty as well.

Loyalty isn't totally dead in America's business. Consider the Stine Seed Company of Adel, Iowa. Harry Stine, the owner and founder, gave all 270 of his employees a Christmas bonus of $1,000 for each year's service. The average check was $4,000 per employee.

Stine said the people were the can-do kind of people who work in the mud and the rain for him. He appreciated their hard work. What he didn't say, but had to feel, was that those employees had been loyal to him and his company. The checks were his way of showing his loyalty to them.

Don't you just know that those workers became more loyal and more hard-working?

Bill Goodwin, of Richmond, VA., owned the AMF Company. He sold the bowling division to Goldman-Sachs in 1996. He had held the bowling business for 10 years. When he sold it, he quadrupled his initial investment. To show his appreciation to the employees for their loyalty, he gave each $1,000 for each year of service. He returned his loyalty in the form of money from his own pocket.

America needs more people like Harry Stine and Bill Goodwin in their boardrooms and executive suites. They both understood loyalty and could help find ways to nurture it. You don't have to be a Harry or a Bill, but you need to figure out the loyalty equation. When you do, your people will feel better, do better jobs, and your results will improve.

Lesson 45

STRACHAN'S LAW

I spent a number of years in the design of production equipment for manufacturing facilities. In doing so I formulated a theory, based upon my experiences, which I called Strachan's Law. It probably has limited value outside of the manufacturing arena, but I include it because it is a valuable lesson I learned in my career. It goes like this:

"If you design a piece of equipment worthy of a Nobel Prize and the plant management team doesn't want it, it will never work. On the other hand, if you design a piece of junk and the plant management team wants it, they will figure out how to make it work."

Don't waste your time on anything that management does not want. It will never work.

Lesson 46

A TALE OF TWO BUSINESSES

In the space of one year I was asked, on two separate occasions, to lead one of our businesses for about three months while the company looked for a permanent leader.

I was extremely excited about these assignments for a personal reason. I had been writing this book while spending time on the road. This project was turning boring evenings at my motel into productive time. When I got my first temporary leadership assignment, I had already written about half of this book. More importantly, I had identified all the chapters and knew exactly what I wanted to write in each. My excitement was rooted in the fact that I was keenly focused on "It Ain't Okay to Fail" and I was being given a wonderful opportunity to apply and test all of these lessons in a real-life experiment.

I knew that I had a scorecard for the experiment. Both businesses had lost money in each of the previous three months. The EBIT (earnings before interest and taxes) would be published at the end of each month and would be the measure of success in applying the lessons I was writing about.

On the morning of my first day at the first business I met with the staff to start sharing my vision, to discuss the culture we would create, and to learn of any concerns they had. I got to the conference room early so that I could have my choice of seating. I deliberately chose a seat that was not at the head of the table. My notes reveal that we discussed the following:

1. The business was losing money. That fact alone said that the business was failing. Working as a team, we would change that because, simply stated, "It ain't okay to fail."

2. As a team, we would review the operating results for the past few months. We would look for opportunities by identifying line items that were out of line with similar businesses. When we found areas that could improve, we would put together plans to improve.

3. It was important that every person in the business see and understand the results. We would have meetings with all employees, including the factory workers, each month to review our results, let everyone know where we were going, and to get their ideas for improvement. These meetings needed to be scheduled over the first few days.

4. Communication throughout the entire business was critical. The monthly "all-employees" meetings would be one method. We would search for and utilize other methods to communicate. I would spend a lot of time in the halls and in the factory on all shifts. My goal would be to meet everyone in the business and to know each person by his or her name.

5. We would have a 30-minute staff meeting every day to review the previous day's results and to review that day's plans.

6. The previous leader's style was autocratic. My style would be enabling. I wanted the managers to adopt my style when dealing with their charges. Management by intimidation would not be tolerated at any level.

7. I would treat everyone with dignity and respect. There would be no yelling. I expected all managers to treat their people with dignity and respect as well. We all would make mistakes. When a mistake happened, the discussion would be civil and would focus on what we might learn from the mistake. Our goal was to not repeat the same mistakes.

8. Even though we were losing money, I would seriously consider every spending request. I would approve those that were necessary to improve the business.

   Reducing costs during rough times was called "costing." I was a firm believer that you can't "cost" your way into prosperity. Purchase orders would be denied if they didn't make sense. They would not be denied if they would improve the business. "Don't be afraid to ask."

9. Complete honesty was essential. I would be completely honest with everyone. I expected everyone to be honest with me.

10. 1 wanted everyone swinging for the fence. We wouldn't turn the business around by trying to lay down a bunt every time we came to the plate. When we swing for the fence, we will strike out at times. Nobody will be in trouble for striking out if they were swinging for the fence and our conversation will focus on what we've learned from that "at-bat." Our objective was to win the game and we would do that even if you don't get on base each time you bat.

11. Speaking of teams, we would function as a team. I wanted a lot of teamwork. I wanted everyone working together on every problem. There are no boundaries, just one big playing field. Sales needed to help solve engineering problems. Finance needed to contribute to solving manufacturing problems.

12. We would also have brief sales productivity meetings each week. They would involve the entire staff and would patch in the home office on the speaker phone. There is no better way to improve a business than winning incremental sales. One way I have found to improve sales is to make everyone a member of the sales team.

13. It was important for me to learn more about the business through the thoughts of each staff member. In order to do that, I would take a staff member to lunch each day until I had spent meaningful time with each of them.

14. I wanted to run the business as if we were all equals. I would sit in various seats around the conference table, but never at the head. If someone comes in, he wouldn't know who the leader was until perhaps we started speaking. If we did it right, it

might not be obvious who the leader was even when we were
speaking!

15. Safety was a primary concern and we would do everything
we could to provide a safe workplace. We would also obey all
laws including federal harassment laws. There would be zero
tolerance and if anyone wanted to get fired, that would be a
good way to make it happen.

16. Housekeeping was important to me. Everyone needed to spend
time keeping their work areas clean and tidy.

As the first few days unfolded, I made certain that I did the things that
I said I would do. I spent a lot of time with staff members and on the
factory floor. I could see the culture changing rapidly and could sense
excitement when talking to the people.

I had a few opportunities to show that I cared about the people. My
predecessor had turned off every other light bulb to reduce the electric
bill. I turned on all the lights and saw the mood change immediately. I
observed an area of the factory where the workers were wearing overcoats
because a heater motor had burned out. It hadn't been replaced in order
to save money. The motor was replaced the very day I observed the
problem. We spent money on light bulbs, a heater motor, and a few
other things that were essential to the business and the people. I watched
the morale and the productivity improve immediately. We had some
"immediate improvement" opportunities and executed them.

We had our "all-employee" meetings during the second week. We chose
to have the meetings during lunch hours and we provided lunch for
everyone.

During the lunches, I shared the business results – revenues, significant
costs, and income. I shared the vision of profitability, answered questions,
and asked for ideas to improve our results.

The entire workforce became energized, motivated, and excited. We
tackled opportunities for improvement and saw immediate results.

At the end of our first month I was proud to announce to everyone in the business that we had turned the corner and had made 7% EBIT. At the end of the second and third months our results had grown to double-digit EBIT's. We celebrated at my last monthly "all-employee" meeting by replacing cold-cut sandwiches with BBQ and catfish meals.

On a personal level, I was pleased that the culture we put in place and the application of my lessons-learned turned the business 180-degrees almost immediately. My replacement kept the same culture and procedures. He grew the business, hired more people, and continued the double-digit profitability. I'm not able to visit that business very often these days, but whenever I do, I get excited about seeing the people and they seem quite happy to see me.

* * * *

Six months later I got the second assignment to lead another business for an interim period.

I was excited because, once again, I had an opportunity to verify the lessons learned of this book. In the previous business I was testing those theories. In this new business, the exercise was to be verification.

Both of the businesses were very similar. Both had been led by an autocrat and both had lost money before I took them over. Both businesses were manufacturing facilities, utilizing similar manufacturing processes. The only difference between the two businesses was that the second business was about three times larger than the first.

I started my assignment in exactly the same way as I had done earlier in the year. I articulated the vision of making the business profitable. I spoke of the culture of teamwork and open communication. In fact, I had the same meetings and used the same talking points I used in the previous business.

The vision, culture change, and meetings excited the people as in the case of the other business. One manager confirmed what I was sensing when she told me that the people "were on fire" with excitement.

We identified opportunities for improving the performance. We made plans and implemented them.

At the end of the first month, our results improved somewhat; however, we were still losing money. At the end of the second month our results were about the same as when we started. By the end of the third month, our results were still no better.

We had successfully identified those operating items that were costing more money than they should. The areas were overtime, indirect labor, downtime, and supplies. We tackled all of these with little success.

It was perplexing to me during those three months and for many months after a permanent replacement was named. Why did the techniques have immediate impact in one business and no apparent impact in a similar business?

I felt terrible. It ain't okay to fail and I did just that. I failed the company and I failed the people in that plant. And I needed to understand why.

The only obvious difference between the two plants was the people themselves. I concluded that the assumption, and flaw, in applying my lessons learned was that the people we encounter in our businesses are both competent and committed to success.

A business can be compared to a race car. The leader is the driver. The engineers are the mechanics and pit crew. Sales people are the fuel and the fuel system. The quality function serves as the wheels. (Watch the wheels come off a business when quality fails.) And the factory workers are the engine.

In order to win the race all of the parts of the car and the racing team must work well. If one part doesn't work well, the race will be lost and the team fails.

If you have a task to turn around a business or to improve its results, you must do the things we did in the two businesses and also evaluate the people as soon as possible. In the second business my managers and I recognized that one staff member was not performing and had to be relieved of his duties. It takes time to evaluate performance and more time to do something about it. A three-month assignment presents a time challenge to evaluate everyone's performance properly.

There were issues with some of the skilled workers that indicated many lacked diagnostic skills and needed a lot of training. Again, it's challenging to identify the people needing training and conduct the training in a three-month time frame.

I mention the time constraints only in the context of understanding why I failed. I am trying to learn from my failure. The time constraint is not offered as an excuse. I failed and it ain't okay. There are no excuses when you fail.

I am also convinced another "people issue" was at play in the second plant. Because of inefficient operations, overtime had become necessary to fulfill all of the orders. Six and seven day operation had become standard. I believe that a very small handful of people had become dependant on overtime pay to meet their financial obligations. This small handful of people had no interest in "fixing" the business. These few people were skillful in dragging their feet. Given time, we could have identified the people issues and corrected them.

Is the "foot-dragging" real or a figment of my imagination? In talking to plant managers in other companies since my temporary assignment, I have learned that many have experienced the foot-dragging syndrome in their plants.

They told me that they solved the problem by not allowing any overtime and letting the people know that, if they didn't produce the orders during normal hours, the customer would go elsewhere and people would lose their jobs.

* * * *

The lesson here is that the people in your organization are the most important ingredient in your business. Many of the lessons learned focus on how to treat the people to get the best results. It is essential that you make certain that you have competent people who are fully committed to the success of the business. You must not assume that the engine in your race car is running on all eight cylinders.

I have concluded from my real-life experiments that my lessons learned provide a great tune-up to an engine that has all eight spark plugs. If one or two plugs are missing or worn, a tune-up won't help much until the bad or missing plugs are first replaced. This can be accomplished with performance evaluations and forced rankings before the race begins or shortly after it starts. You must focus on that as well as doing everything else.

Lesson 47

ENJOY LIFE NOW

One summer my wife and I took a memorable vacation to Puerto Vallarta. When planning the vacation I discovered that we could rent a two-bedroom villa for not much more than the cost of a hotel room. The villa was on a mountainside overlooking the Pacific Ocean and came complete with a private swimming pool, a cook, and a groundskeeper. It was first-class accommodations in every regard.

Since we would have two bedrooms, we invited a few relatives to vacation with us. We took advantage of all the tourist adventures that we could, and on that vacation, paid little attention to our budget. The bottom line was that we spent a little more than we planned but had no regrets. When we returned I called my stock broker and withdrew a few dollars from the money market account to cover our extra expenses.

When I went to the broker's office to pick up my check I said something to the effect that it was to cover some frivolous expenses incurred on vacation.

He said, "Whether you thought it was frivolous or not, it was a good expense. I can't tell you the number of clients I have who have amassed real wealth over their lives and now are old, ill, and unable to enjoy any of their money. My philosophy is to enjoy life now and if that means you have to spend a few dollars of your savings, while you're still able to, then that's what you have to do."

I've thought about that a lot since then and realize that there is a line somewhere separating frivolous from reckless spending. Frugality lies far to the left of the line. As long as you take care of the necessities, save a little for retirement and save a little for a rainy day, there is nothing wrong with spending a little to enjoy life. In fact, that should be your plan.

Then I thought of work and the hours you work each week in order to be successful. Again, there is a line somewhere that divides the hours you work each week. When you cross that line and spend too much time at work, you sacrifice important things that make your life more enjoyable.

Many of the lessons learned in business involve lines or boundaries which, if crossed, put you in jeopardy. Similarly, there are lines in life which, if crossed, put you in jeopardy.

Could it be that life itself can be represented by a series of lines? Some lines are distinct and clearly placed. Others are fuzzy and we're not sure of their exact location on the continuum. We do know that crossing each one jeopardizes something in life.

The line separating honesty and dishonesty is sharply drawn and easily understood. It is not recommended that we cross it in life or business.

The lines separating strengths from weaknesses are fuzzy and we may not be sure where they lie. We learned that if we carry self-confidence to an excess it becomes arrogance. There is a fuzzy line which separates the two and we each must determine where that line lies and be careful not to cross it.

We learned about the imperial or majestic management team. That is the team that crossed a fuzzy line separating modest perks and appropriate behavior from lavish, extravagant perks and childish, unacceptable behavior.

So it is possible to conclude that there are a number of lines in business that we need to learn about, understand and navigate in order to increase the odds of our success. Really, it ain't okay to fail.

In this chapter, we learned of a line which divides our spending patterns and another line dividing the number of hours we work each week. Those lines are fuzzy lines and we're not sure exactly where they lie. In order to enhance our enjoyment of life, it is recommended that we approach the lines and not cross them.

If you concentrate, you can probably identify more lines. An easy one is the line given to us by the police as we cruise the highways. It's clearly defined and posted on signs. If you cross that line you are putting your billfold and perhaps your life, in jeopardy.

Speaking of life, doesn't medical science give us lines for cholesterol and blood pressure which, if we cross, put us in danger of stroke and heart disease?

What better way to close than to give you a few questions to ponder long after you put this book on the shelf.

Is there a branch of psychology, yet to be developed or understood, that deals with the theory of life's "lines"?

Is it possible that the secret to life and the secret of business success lie in understanding the "theory of lines," what they are, where they lie, getting as close to them as possible, and never crossing them?

Available in early 2007

IT AIN'T OKAY TO FAIL

AND OTHER POWERFUL
LESSONS LEARNED

IN SALES
AND
MARKETING

Printed in the United States
52412LVS00004B/130-141